Raspberry Pi Android Projects

Create exciting projects by connecting Raspberry Pi to your Android phone

Gökhan Kurt

[PACKT] open source *
PUBLISHING   community experience distilled

BIRMINGHAM - MUMBAI

Raspberry Pi Android Projects

First published: September 2015

Production reference: 2141215

Published by Packt Publishing Ltd.
Livery Place
35 Livery Street
Birmingham B3 2PB, UK.

ISBN 978-1-78588-702-4

www.packtpub.com

Credits

Author
Gökhan Kurt

Reviewers
Thushara Jayawardena
Wolf Paulus
Eric Wuehler

Commissioning Editor
Nadeem Bagban

Acquisition Editor
Vivek Anantharaman

Content Development Editor
Arwa Manasawala

Technical Editor
Rahul C. Shah

Copy Editor
Sonia Cheema

Project Coordinator
Shweta H Birwatkar

Proofreader
Safis Editing

Indexer
Monica Ajmera Mehta

Production Coordinator
Arvindkumar Gupta

Cover Work
Arvindkumar Gupta

About the Author

Gökhan Kurt has been trying to keep up with the latest developments in technology and IT in his 15-year-long development career. For the past 4 years, he has been working at IFS Labs, one of the top innovation departments of the Swedish software industry. Currently, he is involved in the Internet of Things and has been developing prototype IoT implementations using Raspberry Pi.

He has a master's of science degree from Chalmers University of Technology and a bachelor's degree from the Middle East Technical University. You can connect with him on Twitter (@KurtGok) and on LinkedIn (http://se.linkedin.com/in/kurtgokhan).

I would like to thank my dear wife, Hediye, for her patience during the writing of this book. Special thanks to my 3-year-old son, Derin, for providing me with the intellectual support needed for writing this book with his Lego building skills. I would also like to thank my 3-month-old daughter, Eliz, for keeping me awake at night so that I was able to think about exciting projects to include in this book.

About the Reviewers

Thushara Jayawardena is in his fourteenth year of working in the software development industry. Right after he graduated from university in 2001, he joined the IFS world operations (http://www.ifsworld.com/) development center in Colombo, Sri Lanka. His early years were spent as a junior SW engineer. He then moved into SW systems as a system engineer, overseeing mission-critical production systems. During this time, he became a principal systems engineer, and also moved to Sweden in 2007 where he started working at the head office of IFS in Linköping, Sweden. From 2014 to date, he has been working on product benchmarking for IFS. He has mainly worked with technologies, such as Oracle RDBMS, J2EE systems, and Jboss/Oracle WebLogic. He is also knowledgeable about various scripting technologies and languages, such as PowerShell and VB scripting. In recent years, he's been active in monitoring tools written in Angular JS and Google graphs. In the field of product benchmarking, he has worked with data science, especially generating synthetic data for load simulations. He has also spent considerable time at work on performance testing tools, such as HP LoadRunner.

In his spare time, apart from travelling and enjoying different cultures with his son, daughter, and wife, he spends time with Android, Google App Engine, and Raspberry Pi home-brewing projects.

Eric Wuehler lives in the Pacific Northwest with his lovely wife and three children. He has been working in the technology field professionally for over 20 years. He can be reached online at ericwuehler.com.

www.PacktPub.com

Support files, eBooks, discount offers, and more

For support files and downloads related to your book, please visit www.PacktPub.com.

Did you know that Packt offers eBook versions of every book published, with PDF and ePub files available? You can upgrade to the eBook version at www.PacktPub.com and as a print book customer, you are entitled to a discount on the eBook copy. Get in touch with us at service@packtpub.com for more details.

At www.PacktPub.com, you can also read a collection of free technical articles, sign up for a range of free newsletters and receive exclusive discounts and offers on Packt books and eBooks.

https://www2.packtpub.com/books/subscription/packtlib

Do you need instant solutions to your IT questions? PacktLib is Packt's online digital book library. Here, you can search, access, and read Packt's entire library of books.

Why subscribe?

- Fully searchable across every book published by Packt
- Copy and paste, print, and bookmark content
- On demand and accessible via a web browser

Free access for Packt account holders

If you have an account with Packt at www.PacktPub.com, you can use this to access PacktLib today and view 9 entirely free books. Simply use your login credentials for immediate access.

Table of Contents

Preface

The most popular gadget in the maker community, *Raspberry Pi*, and the most popular smartphone OS, *Android*, combine their powers in this book, resulting in exciting, useful, and easy-to-follow projects. The projects covered come in handy in your daily interaction with the Pi and can be helpful as building blocks for even more amazing projects.

What this book covers

Chapter 1, Make a Remote Desktop Connection to Your Pi from Anywhere, teaches you how to make the initial setup to get started with your Pi and connect remotely to the Pi desktop from an Android device from anywhere in the world.

Chapter 2, Server Management with Pi, builds on the previous chapter to manage the Pi and the different servers we install on it. We will even introduce an interesting, useful project on the way that makes use of these servers.

Chapter 3, Live Streaming of a Surveillance Camera from the Pi, shows you how to turn your Pi into a webcam and then introduces you to the techniques to use it in surveillance mode, which is accessible through an Android device and the Internet.

Chapter 4, Turn Your Pi into a Media Center, shows you how you can turn your Pi into a media center that is controllable from an Android device.

Chapter 5, Missed Calls with Pi, introduces the techniques required to access sensors and components on the Pi from Android through Bluetooth and shows how the Pi can notify you about the calls you receive on your phone.

Chapter 6, The Vehicle Pi, helps you connect the Pi to your car and follow it from your Android phone.

What you need for this book

All the software used in this book is freely available on the Internet. You need Raspberry Pi 2 and an Android device. In some chapters, we will even use a USB Wi-Fi dongle, DHT11 or DHT22 temperature sensor, jumper cables, an LED light, a USB Bluetooth dongle, Pi camera, USB GPS receiver, and an OBD Bluetooth interface, all of which are available on online stores.

Who this book is for

Raspberry Pi Android Projects targets those of you who want to create engaging and useful projects with the Pi, which are controllable through an Android phone. No prior knowledge of Pi or Android is required. At the end of each chapter, you will have succeeded in creating a project that can be used daily, and will be equipped with skills that could help you develop even more exciting projects in the future. The projects covered in this book will contain some minor programming steps and these steps will be described in detail even for the most inexperienced readers.

Conventions

In this book, you will find a number of text styles that distinguish between different kinds of information. Here are some examples of these styles and an explanation of their meaning.

Code words in text, database table names, folder names, filenames, file extensions, pathnames, dummy URLs, user input, and Twitter handles are shown as follows: "The next step is to install a component called x11vnc."

A block of code is set as follows:

```
network={
    ssid="THE ID OF THE NETWORK YOU WANT TO CONNECT"
    psk="PASSWORD OF YOUR WIFI"
}
```

Any command-line input or output is written as follows:

```
sudo apt-get install apache2
sudo apt-get install php5 libapache2-mod-php5
sudo apt-get install libapache2-mod-auth-mysql php5-mysql
```

New terms and **important words** are shown in bold. Words that you see on the screen, for example, in menus or dialog boxes, appear in the text like this: "Initiate the connection by pressing the **Connect** button, and you should now be able to see the Pi desktop on your Android device."

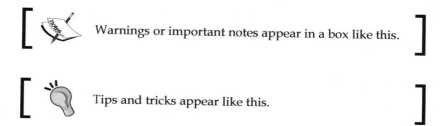

> Warnings or important notes appear in a box like this.

> Tips and tricks appear like this.

Reader feedback

Feedback from our readers is always welcome. Let us know what you think about this book—what you liked or disliked. Reader feedback is important for us as it helps us develop titles that you will really get the most out of.

To send us general feedback, simply e-mail feedback@packtpub.com, and mention the book's title in the subject of your message.

If there is a topic that you have expertise in and you are interested in either writing or contributing to a book, see our author guide at www.packtpub.com/authors.

Customer support

Now that you are the proud owner of a Packt book, we have a number of things to help you to get the most from your purchase.

Downloading the example code

You can download the example code files from your account at http://www.packtpub.com for all the Packt Publishing books you have purchased. If you purchased this book elsewhere, you can visit http://www.packtpub.com/support and register to have the files e-mailed directly to you. You can also download the code bundle of this book from https://github.com/kurtng/Raspberry-Pi-Android-Projects.

Downloading the color images of this book

We also provide you with a PDF file that has color images of the screenshots/diagrams used in this book. The color images will help you better understand the changes in the output. You can download this file from https://www.packtpub.com/sites/default/files/downloads/Raspberry_Pi_Android_Projects_ColoredImages.pdf.

Errata

Although we have taken every care to ensure the accuracy of our content, mistakes do happen. If you find a mistake in one of our books — maybe a mistake in the text or the code — we would be grateful if you could report this to us. By doing so, you can save other readers from frustration and help us improve subsequent versions of this book. If you find any errata, please report them by visiting http://www.packtpub.com/submit-errata, selecting your book, clicking on the **Errata Submission Form** link, and entering the details of your errata. Once your errata are verified, your submission will be accepted and the errata will be uploaded to our website or added to any list of existing errata under the Errata section of that title.

To view the previously submitted errata, go to https://www.packtpub.com/books/content/support and enter the name of the book in the search field. The required information will appear under the **Errata** section.

Piracy

Piracy of copyrighted material on the Internet is an ongoing problem across all media. At Packt, we take the protection of our copyright and licenses very seriously. If you come across any illegal copies of our works in any form on the Internet, please provide us with the location address or website name immediately so that we can pursue a remedy.

Please contact us at copyright@packtpub.com with a link to the suspected pirated material.

We appreciate your help in protecting our authors and our ability to bring you valuable content.

Questions

If you have a problem with any aspect of this book, you can contact us at questions@packtpub.com, and we will do our best to address the problem.

1

Make a Remote Desktop Connection to Your Pi from Anywhere

In this project, we will make a gentle introduction to both Pi and Android platforms to warm us up. Many users of the Pi face similar problems when they wish to administer it. You have to be near your Pi and connect a screen and a keyboard to it. We will solve this everyday problem by remotely connecting to our Pi desktop interface. The chapter covers following topics:

- Prerequisites
- Installing Linux in your Pi
- Making necessary changes in settings
- Installing necessary components in the Pi and Android
- Connecting the Pi and Android

Prerequisites

The following items are used throughout this chapter and will be needed to complete the project:

- **Raspberry Pi 2 Model B**: This is the latest addition to the Raspberry Pi family. It has replaced the previous Pi 1 Model B+. The previous model should work fine for the purpose of the projects covered in this book.
- **MicroSD card**: The Raspberry Pi Foundation recommends using an 8 GB class 6 microSD card.

- **Android device**: The device should have at least a 1.5 or higher Android version, which is required by the app used in this chapter. In some of the exciting projects that follow, we will need Android 4.3 or later versions.

- **HDMI cable**: This will be used to connect the Pi to a screen for initial set up.

- **Ethernet cable**: This will be used for network connections.

- **Computer**: This will be used to copy the Raspbian OS on to the microSD card.

- **USB mouse**: This will be used during initial setup.

The following image shows the Raspberry Pi 2 Model B:

Raspberry Pi 2 Model B

Installing Linux on your Pi

We will use **Raspbian** as the operating system on our Pi. My choice is solely based on the fact that it is recommended by the Raspberry Pi Foundation. It is based on the Debian version of Linux and optimized for Raspberry Pi hardware. Apart from being the most used operating system for Raspberry Pi, it contains almost 35,000 packages, such as games, mail servers, office suite, internet browsers and so on. At the time of writing this book, the latest release was dated May 5, 2015.

There are two main ways of installing Raspbian. You can either use the OS image as a whole or you can begin with an easy-to-use tool-operating system bundle called **NOOBS**. We will cover both cases here.

 There are SD cards for sale with NOOBS or Raspbian already installed. It might be a good idea to get one of these and skip the OS installation part of this chapter.

However, before we begin, we might need to format our SD card as previous OS installations may corrupt the card. You'll notice this if only a fraction of free space on the card is shown to be available even though you have formatted the card using the formatting utility provided by your computer's OS. The tool we will use is called the **SD Formatter** and is available for Mac and Windows from **SD Association** at `https://www.sdcard.org/downloads/formatter_4/index.html`. Install and start it. You will see the following interface asking you to select the SD card location:

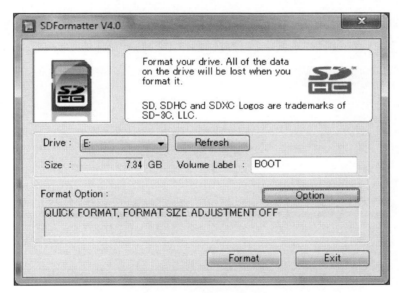

The SD Formatter interface

Installing using NOOBS

The latest version of NOOBS can be found at `http://downloads.raspberrypi.org/NOOBS_latest`. Download and extract the contents on to the SD card. Attach the card to your Pi and connect it to a screen using an HDMI cable. Do not forget to connect the USB mouse. When the Pi is attached to a power source, you will be presented with a list of choices you can make. Check the **Raspbian** installation option on the list, and then click on **Install**. This will install Raspbian on your SD card and restart the Pi.

Installing using a Raspbian image

The latest version of the Raspbian OS can be found at `http://downloads.raspberrypi.org/raspbian_latest`. The ZIP file is almost 1 GB in size and contains a single file with an `.img` extension, which is 3.2 GB in size. Unzip the contents and follow the steps in the next section to extract it to a suitable microSD card.

Extracting the OS image to an SD card

To extract an image file, we need a disk imaging utility and we will use a freely available one called **Win32 Disk Imager** on Windows. It can be downloaded at `http://sourceforge.net/projects/win32diskimager/`. On Mac OS, there is a similar tool called **ApplePi Baker** available at `http://www.tweaking4all.com/hardware/raspberry-pi/macosx-apple-pi-baker/`. Download and install it on to your computer. The installation will contain an executable file, `Win32DiskImager`, which you should start in the administrator mode by right clicking on it and selecting **Run as administrator**.

In the **Win32 Disk Imager** window, you should choose the image file you've extracted and the drive for SD card similar to what is shown in the following screenshot:

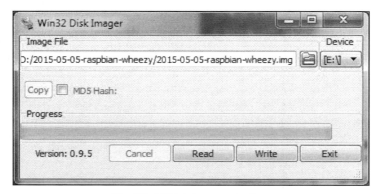

The Win32 Disk Imager window

Clicking on the **Write** button will start the process and your SD card will be ready to be inserted into the Pi.

Making necessary changes in settings

When the Pi is still plugged into a screen with HDMI, connect it to a network using Ethernet. The first time the Pi starts, you will be presented with a settings utility as shown in the following screenshot:

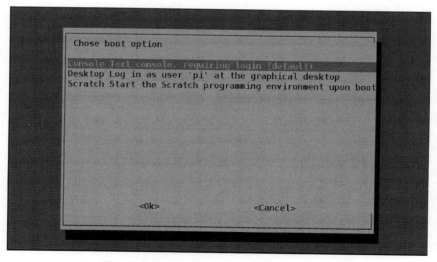

Raspberry Pi Software Configuration Tool

You can optionally select the first option in the list to **Expand Filesystem**. Select the third option as well to **Enable Boot to Desktop**.

In the following menu, select the second item in the list which is **Desktop Log in as user 'pi' at the graphical desktop**. Then, choose **<Finish>** and select **Yes** to reboot the device.

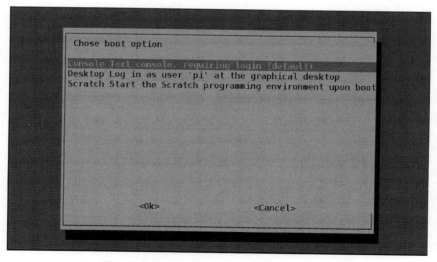

Choose desktop startup in the configuration tool

After reboot, you will be presented with the Raspbian's default desktop manager environment called **LXDE**.

Installing necessary components in the Pi and Android

As the following screenshot shows the LXDE desktop manager comes with an initial setup and a few preinstalled programs:

The LXDE desktop management environment

By clicking on the screen image on the tab bar located at the top, you will be able to open a terminal screen that we will use to send commands to the Pi.

The next step is to install a component called x11vnc. This is a VNC server for X, the window management component of Linux. Issue the following command on the terminal:

```
sudo apt-get install x11vnc
```

This will download and install x11vnc to the Pi. We can even set a password to be used by VNC clients that will remote desktop to this Pi using the following command and provide a password to be used later on:

```
x11vnc -storepasswd
```

Next, we can get the x11vnc server running whenever the Pi is rebooted and the LXDE desktop manager starts. This can be done through the following steps:

1. Go into the .config directory on the Pi user's home directory located at /home/pi:

    ```
    cd /home/pi/.config
    ```

2. Make a subdirectory here named autostart:

    ```
    mkdir autostart
    ```

3. Go into the autostart directory:

    ```
    cd autostart
    ```

4. Start editing a file named x11vnc.desktop. As a terminal editor, I am using nano, which is the easiest one to use on the Pi for novice users, but there are more exciting alternatives, such as **vi**:

    ```
    nano x11vnc.desktop
    ```

    Add the following content into this file:

    ```
    [Desktop Entry]
    Encoding=UTF-8
    Type=Application
    Name=X11VNC
    Comment=
    Exec=x11vnc -forever -usepw -display :0 -ultrafilexfer
    StartupNotify=false
    Terminal=false
    Hidden=false
    ```

5. Save and exit using (*Ctrl+X, Y, Enter*) in order if you are using **nano** as the editor of your choice.

6. Now you should reboot the Pi to get the server running using the following command:

    ```
    sudo reboot
    ```

After rebooting using the `sudo reboot` command, we can now find out what IP address our Pi has been given in the terminal window by issuing the `ifconfig` command. The IP address assigned to your Pi is to be found under the `eth0` entry and is given after the `inet addr` keyword. Write this address down:

```
pi@raspberrypi ~ $ ifconfig
eth0      Link encap:Ethernet  HWaddr b8:27:eb:da:48:11
          inet addr:192.168.1.16  Bcast:192.168.1.255  Mask:255.255.255.0
          UP BROADCAST RUNNING MULTICAST  MTU:1500  Metric:1
          RX packets:219 errors:0 dropped:0 overruns:0 frame:0
          TX packets:103 errors:0 dropped:0 overruns:0 carrier:0
          collisions:0 txqueuelen:1000
          RX bytes:30908 (30.1 KiB)  TX bytes:15261 (14.9 KiB)

lo        Link encap:Local Loopback
          inet addr:127.0.0.1  Mask:255.0.0.0
          UP LOOPBACK RUNNING  MTU:65536  Metric:1
          RX packets:72 errors:0 dropped:0 overruns:0 frame:0
          TX packets:72 errors:0 dropped:0 overruns:0 carrier:0
          collisions:0 txqueuelen:0
          RX bytes:6288 (6.1 KiB)  TX bytes:6288 (6.1 KiB)

wlan0     Link encap:Ethernet  HWaddr 00:0f:60:04:66:df
          UP BROADCAST MULTICAST  MTU:1500  Metric:1
          RX packets:0 errors:0 dropped:0 overruns:0 frame:0
          TX packets:0 errors:0 dropped:0 overruns:0 carrier:0
          collisions:0 txqueuelen:1000
          RX bytes:0 (0.0 B)  TX bytes:0 (0.0 B)

pi@raspberrypi ~ $
```

Example output from the ifconfig command

7.   The next step is to download a VNC client to your Android device.

In this project, we will use a freely available client for Android, namely **androidVNC** or as it is named in the Play Store—**VNC Viewer for Android** by **androidVNC team + antlersoft**. The latest version in use at the writing of this book was 0.5.0.

Note that in order to be able to connect your Android VNC client to the Pi, both the Pi and the Android device should be connected to the same network—Android through Wi-Fi, and Pi through its Ethernet port.

Connecting the Pi and Android

Install and open androidVNC on your device. You will be presented with a first activity user interface asking for the details of the connection. Here, you should provide **Nickname** for the connection, **Password** you enter when you run the x11vnc -storepasswd command, and the IP **Address** of the Pi that you found out using the ifconfig command. Initiate the connection by pressing the **Connect** button, and you should now be able to see the Pi desktop on your Android device.

In androidVNC, you should be able to move the mouse pointer by clicking on the screen and under the options menu in the androidVNC app, you will find out how to send text and keys to the Pi with the help of *Enter* and *Backspace*.

> You may even find it convenient to connect to the Pi from another computer. I recommend using RealVNC for this purpose, which is available on Windows, Linux, and Mac OS.

What if I want to use Wi-Fi on the Pi?

In order to use a Wi-Fi dongle on the Pi, first of all, open the wpa_supplicant configuration file using the nano editor with the following command:

```
sudo nano /etc/wpa_supplicant/wpa_supplicant.conf
```

Add the following to the end of this file:

```
network={
    ssid="THE ID OF THE NETWORK YOU WANT TO CONNECT"
    psk="PASSWORD OF YOUR WIFI"
}
```

> I assume that you have set up your wireless home network to use WPA-PSK as the authentication mechanism. If you have another mechanism, you should refer to the wpa_supplicant documentation. LXDE provides even better ways to connect to Wi-Fi networks through a GUI. It can be found on the upper-right corner of the desktop environment on the Pi.

Connecting from anywhere

Now, we have connected to the Pi from our device, which we need to connect to the same network as the Pi. However, most of us would like to connect to the Pi from around the world as well. To do this, first of all, we need to now the IP address of the home network assigned to us by our network provider. By going to `http://whatismyipaddress.com` URL, we can figure out what our home network's IP address is. The next step is to log in to our router and open up requests to the Pi from around the world. For this purpose, we will use a functionality found on most modern routers called **port forwarding**.

> Be aware of the risks contained in port forwarding. You are opening up access to your Pi from all around the world, even to malicious users. I strongly recommend that you change the default password of the user `pi` before performing this step. You can change passwords using the `passwd` command.

By logging onto the router's management portal and navigating to the **Port Forwarding** tab, we can open up requests to the Pi's internal network IP address, which we have figured out previously, and the default port of the VNC server, which is `5900`. Now, we can provide our external IP address to androidVNC from anywhere around the world instead of an internal IP address that works only if we are on the same network as the Pi.

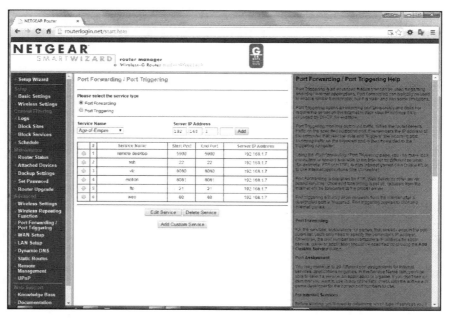

Port Forwarding settings on Netgear router administration page

Refer to your router's user manual to see how to change the **Port Forwarding** settings. Most routers require you to connect through the Ethernet port in order to access the management portal instead of Wi-Fi.

Problems with dynamic LAN IP addresses and external IP addresses

There is one minor problem with this setup. The Pi might get a new LAN IP address each time you restart it, making the **Port Forwarding** setting useless. To avoid this, most routers provide the **Address Reservation** setting. You can tell most routers that each time a device with a unique MAC address is connected, it should get the same IP address.

Another problem is that your **Internet Service Provider (ISP)** might assign new IP addresses to you each time you restart your router or for any other reason. You can use a dynamic DNS service, such as DynDNS, to avoid such problems. Most routers are capable of using dynamic DNS services. Alternatively, you can get a static IP address by contacting your ISP.

Summary

In this project, we installed Raspbian, warmed up with the Pi, enabled the desktop environment on it, and connected to the Pi using an Android device.

In the next chapter, we will access the console of the Pi directly and even transfer files to and from it using FTP from our Android devices.

2
Server Management with Pi

In the first half of this project, we will move from a desktop-based console to a text-based one that gives more power to the user and lets you perform more advanced tasks compared to the desktop. We will access the Pi's Linux console from an Android device and control it remotely. In the second half, we will send and receive files between the Pi and Android through FTP. We will even combine the two parts by managing our newly installed FTP server remotely using the text-based console. In this chapter, we will even install database and web servers on to the Pi to show how to manage them later on. To make it even more fun, we will implement a simple but useful mini project that makes use of both web and database servers. The following topics will be covered:

- Remote console to the Pi from Android
- Exchanging files between the Pi and Android
- A simple database and web server implementation
- Simple management of servers

Remote console to the Pi from Android

The administrators of Linux and Unix computers have been using text-based command-line interfaces called **shell** for many years to manage and administer their servers. As the Pi's OS, Raspbian, is a Linux variant, the most natural way to access and issue commands or check the status of running programs, services, and different servers on the Pi is again by issuing commands on this text-based shell. There are different shell implementations but the one that is used on Raspbian by default is **bash**. The most well-known way of accessing shell remotely on a Linux server is through the **Secure Shell** protocol known, in general, as **SSH**.

Secure Shell (SSH) is an encrypted network protocol used to send shell commands to a remote machine in a secure way. SSH does two things for you. It enables, through different tools, such as the ones we will present to you in a moment, you to send commands to the remote machine and it does this using a secure channel established over an insecure network.

For SSH to work, there should be an SSH server already running that can accept and respond to SSH client requests. On Raspberry Pi, this feature is enabled by default. If by any means, it is disabled, you can enable it using the Pi configuration program by issuing the following command:

```
sudo raspi-config
```

Then, navigate to **ssh** and hit *Enter*, and then select **Enable or disable ssh server**.

On the client side, and as we are using Android as our client throughout this book, we will download an app called ConnectBot. It is one of the most popular SSH clients on Android and the latest version as of today is 1.8.4. Download it to your device and open it.

You will need to provide the username and IP address that we found out in the previous chapter. We do not need to provide the port as ConnectBot will use the default port for SSH in this case. Click on **Yes** if you are asked to continue with the connection because of problems with the authenticity of the host. You are asked this question because you are connecting to the Pi for the first time through a remote SSH.

Note that in the following screenshot, I have provided the internal IP address of my home network. You might want to use an external IP address and connect to the Pi from outside your home network. For this purpose, you'll need to add the standard FTP ports 21 and 20 to your port forwarding settings as well. The same applies to the SSH protocol, which has a default port number of 22.

As we have discussed earlier, there is a security risk in opening ports this way and also keeping the default password for the user pi on the Pi.

The following screenshot illustrates connection details on ConnectBot:

Connection details on ConnectBot

Now, provide the default password for the `pi` account, which is `raspberry`, or the one you have changed it to. After this step, you will be connected to the Pi remotely using SSH, as seen in the following screenshot:

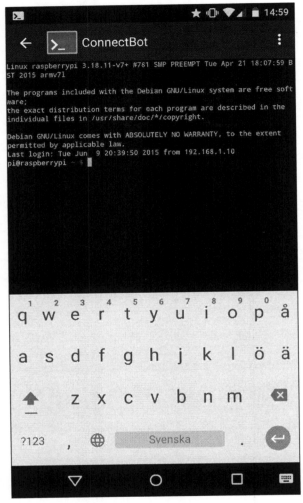

The prompt provided by ConnectBot

You are now ready to issue commands on your Pi and check the status of different services. This connection will be saved with all its properties. Next time you want to log in, you will not need to provide an address, username, and password information.

 On a Mac or Linux, you can use the ssh command installed on your system by default. On Windows, you can download PuTTY to issue the same commands as the ones in ConnectBot.

Exchanging files between the Pi and Android

In the second part of this chapter, we will use the Pi as an FTP server to share files between our Android devices or send files to the Pi to view them on a larger screen that you connect to the Pi HDMI port. The FTP server we will use is vsftpd. It is a lightweight FTP server used in many small projects. To install it on our Pi, we use the following command:

```
sudo apt-get install vsftpd
```

The preceding command will even start the FTP service.

However, we should make some changes in the configuration of the FTP server to use it effectively. For this purpose, we need to edit the FTP server configuration file using this command:

```
sudo nano /etc/vsftpd.conf
```

Find the two lines containing #local_enable=YES and #write_enable=YES and remove the # comment sign at the beginning of these lines before you save and exit. These changes will enable the user pi to login and be able to send files to the Pi. To restart the FTP server, issue this command:

```
sudo service vsftpd restart
```

Now, we need to install an FTP client on Android. For this purpose, we will use **AndFTP**. It is enough to use the free version for our project. We see the following initial view on the Android device after opening it:

An initial view of the AndFTP client

Pressing the plus button will take you to the following view, where you will be asked for connection properties:

Connection properties on AndFTP

Provide the IP address of the Pi you found out in the first chapter, pi as username, and raspberry as the password or the one you have changed to. Then, scroll down to the end of the view and press the **Save** button. This will save the connection properties and send you back to the main view:

The list of connections in AndFTP

Clicking on the newly created connection, shown as a blue folder, will initiate the FTP connection to the Pi and log the user `pi` in. This will get you into the `home` directory for the `pi` user, as shown in the following screenshot:

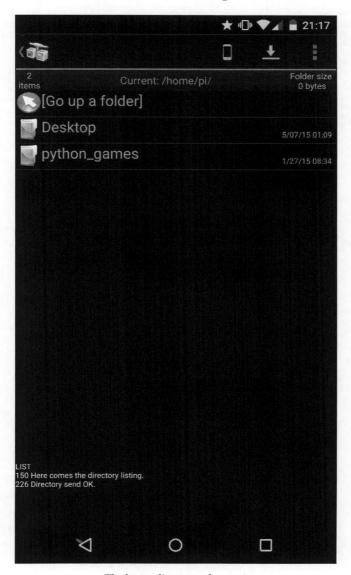

The home directory of user pi

Now you will be able to upload files from your Android device to the Pi by pressing the mobile phone-like icon in AndFTP and choosing a file to upload afterwards. You can set up AndFTP from another Android device on the same network or even another computer using a built-in FTP client, and download the newly uploaded file to view it; this way, you have shared your first file between different Android clients using Raspberry Pi as an FTP server.

A simple database and web server implementation

Next, we'll take our project one step further and install both a database and web server, which we can administer later on using ConnectBot. We will even make it more fun by implementing a real project that makes use of these servers. The best candidate for this purpose is a sensor measurement scenario. We will connect a temperature/humidity sensor to our Pi and save the measurements into a database that we will install on the Pi, which a web server will make available to clients. We can later on manage these servers remotely, which is the main objective in this chapter.

Connecting the sensor

For the purpose of this project, we will use a sensor, **DHT11**, which measures both temperature and humidity, but for the sake of easier connections, we will use an off-the-shelf module called **Keyes DHT11** or DHT11 for short, which contains these sensors.

 There is even an improved version of DHT11, which is DHT22. It costs a little bit more but has more accurate sensors on it.

Using this sensor module instead of the sensors itself will enable us to connect the sensors to the Pi using only three jumper wires and without a breadboard or resistor. There is another advantage of using this module instead of the sensors: the sensors provide analog data that the Pi cannot handle. Pi is capable of handling digital information on its GPIO ports. The DHT11 module does the conversion for us. The following image illustrates the DHT11 sensor module along with a description of the pins associated with it:

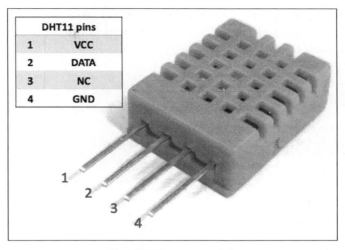

The DHT11 sensor module

The following image illustrates the Keyes DHT11 sensor module:

The Keyes DHT11 sensor module

Now, connect the **GND** output from the sensor module to Pi's GPIO Ground, **5V** output to Pi's 5V pin, and **DATA** to Pi's **GPIO-4** pin. The following diagram shows the layout of Pi's GPIO pins and their names:

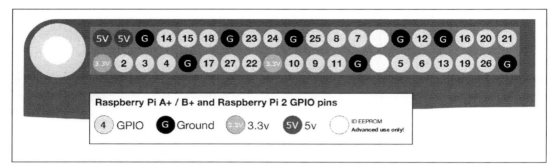

Raspberry Pi GPIO pin layout

The next step is to read the values these sensors provide. For this purpose, we will use a widely used library from **Adafruit**, which is specially designed for these kinds of sensors developed in the Python programming language. Before we can use it, we need to install some software components to our Raspberry Pi.

Firstly, we need to update our Pi and install some dependencies using these commands:

```
sudo apt-get update
sudo apt-get install build-essential python-dev
```

The sensor library itself is on GitHub and we will download it from there onto our Pi using the following command:

```
git clone https://github.com/adafruit/Adafruit_Python_DHT.git
```

This command downloads the library and saves it in a subdirectory. Now, go into this subdirectory using the following command:

```
cd Adafruit_Python_DHT
```

Next, you need to actually install the sensor library using the following command:

```
sudo python setup.py install
```

Here, we use the standard Python third-party module install functionality, which installs the Adafruit library globally onto your system at the standard Python library install location, /usr/local/lib/python2.7/dist-packages/. This is why we need superuser privileges, which we can get using sudo command.

Now we are ready to begin reading measurements from the sensor using the example code that we downloaded together with the library. Assuming that you are still in the `Adafruit_Python_DHT` directory, the following command does the job:

```
sudo ./examples/AdafruitDHT.py 11 4
```

In this command, `11` is the descriptor used to identify DHT11 sensor and `4` denotes the GPIO pin 4. You should now get an output that looks like this:

```
Temp=25.0*C  Humidity=36.0%
```

Installing the database

After verifying that the sensor and connections to the Pi work, we will save the measurements in a database. The database we will use is MySQL. Use the following command to install MySQL to the Pi:

```
sudo apt-get install mysql-server python-mysqldb
```

During the installation, you will be asked to set a password for the administrator account root. I will set admin as the password and refer to it in the upcoming code. The following command takes you into the MySQL shell where you can issue SQL commands, such as inserting data into a database or querying data already in the database. You should provide the password you have set when you're asked for it:

```
mysql -u root -p
```

You can exit from the MySQL shell anytime using the `exit` command.

The next step in the MySQL shell is to create a database and use it for any further SQL statement that follow:

```
mysql> CREATE DATABASE measurements;
mysql> USE measurements;
```

The following SQL statement will create a table in this newly created database that we will use to save sensor measurements:

```
mysql> CREATE TABLE measurements (ttime DATETIME, temperature
NUMERIC(4,1), humidity NUMERIC(4,1));
```

The next step is to implement a Python script that reads from our sensor and saves it to the database. Put the following code in a file with the name sense.py under the home directory using the previously discussed nano command. You can use the cd command without parameters to go back to the home directory from any place in the pi directory structure. Note an important fact that the file should not contain any empty preceding lines, which means that the line referring to the Python command should be the first line in the file. The following code forms the content of our sense.py file:

```python
#!/usr/bin/python

import sys
import Adafruit_DHT
import MySQLdb

humidity, temperature = Adafruit_DHT.read_retry(Adafruit_DHT.DHT11,
4)
#temperature = temperature * 1.8 + 32 # fahrenheit
print str(temperature) + " " + str(humidity)
if humidity is not None and temperature is not None:
    db = MySQLdb.connect("localhost", "root", "admin",
"measurements")
    curs = db.cursor()
    try:
        sqlline = "insert into measurements values(NOW(),
{0:0.1f},
{1:0.1f});".format(temperature, humidity)
        curs.execute(sqlline)
        curs.execute ("DELETE FROM measurements WHERE ttime <
NOW() - INTERVAL 180 DAY;")
        db.commit()
        print "Data committed"
    except MySQLdb.Error as e:
        print "Error: the database is being rolled back" + str(e)
        db.rollback()
else:
    print "Failed to get reading. Try again!"
```

You should change the password parameter in the MySQLdb.connect method call to the one you have assigned to the root user on the MySQL server. You should even consider creating a new user with access to just the measurements table for security reasons, as the root user has full access to the database. Refer to the MySQL documentation for this purpose.

The next step is to change the file properties and make it an executable file with the following command:

```
chmod +x sense.py
```

Note that this script saves only a single measurement. We need to schedule the running of this script. For this purpose, we will use a built-in Linux utility called **cron**, which allows tasks to be automatically run in the background at regular intervals by the cron daemon. **crontab,** also known as CRON TABle, is a file that contains the schedule of cron entries to be run at specified times. By running the following command, we can edit this table:

```
crontab -e
```

Add the following line to this file and save it. This will make the cron deamon run our script once every five minutes:

```
*/5 * * * * sudo /home/pi/sense.py
```

Installing the web server

Now, we will save our measurements into the database. The next step is to view them in a web browser using a web server. For this purpose, we will use **Apache** as the web server and **PHP** as the programming language. To install Apache and the packages required for our purpose, run the following commands:

```
sudo apt-get install apache2
sudo apt-get install php5 libapache2-mod-php5
sudo apt-get install libapache2-mod-auth-mysql php5-mysql
```

Then, change your directory to the web server's default directory:

```
cd /var/www
```

Here, we will create a file that will be accessed by users through the web server we have installed. The file is executed by the web server and the result of this execution is sent to the clients connected. We will name it `index.php`:

```
sudo nano index.php
```

The contents should look like the following code. Here, you should again change the password for the MySQL user root to the one you have chosen in the call to the `new mysqli` constructor method:

```php
<?php

// Create connection
```

```php
$conn = new mysqli("localhost", "root", "admin", "measurements");
// Check connection
if ($conn->connect_error) {
    die("Connection failed: " . $conn->connect_error);
}

$sql = "SELECT ttime, temperature, humidity FROM measurements
WHERE ttime > NOW() - INTERVAL 3 DAY;";
$result = $conn->query($sql);
?>
<html>
<head>
<!-- Load c3.css -->
<link href="https://rawgit.com/masayuki0812/c3/master/c3.min.css"
rel="stylesheet" type="text/css">

<!-- Load d3.js and c3.js -->
<script src="https://rawgit.com/mbostock/d3/master/d3.min.js"
charset="utf-8"></script>
<script src="https://rawgit.com/masayuki0812/c3/master/c3.min.js"></
scrip>
</head>
<body>
<div id="chart"></div>

<script>

<?php

if($result->num_rows > 0) {
?>
var json = [
<?php
  while($row = $result->fetch_assoc()) {
    ?>{ttime:'<?=$row["ttime"]?>',temperature:<?=$row["temperature"]?>
,humidity:<?=$row["humidity"]?>},<?
  }
}
?>
];
<?php
$conn->close();
?>
var chart = c3.generate({
    bindto: '#chart',
```

```
data: {
  x: 'ttime',
  xFormat: '%Y-%m-%d %H:%M:%S',
  keys: {
    x:'ttime',
    value: ['temperature', 'humidity']
  },
  json: json,
  axes: {
    temperature: 'y',
    humidity: 'y2'
  }
},
axis: {
    x: {
        type: 'timeseries',
        tick: {
            format: '%Y-%m-%d %H:%M'
        }
    },
    y: {
        label: 'temperature'
    },
    y2: {
        show: true,
        label: 'humidity'
    }
  }
});
</script>
</body>
</html>
```

We want this page to be the default start page that web browsers get whenever they access the server directly with only an IP address. You can back up the old default start page for Apache as follows:

```
sudo mv index.html oldindex.html
```

Navigating to the IP address of the Pi from a browser will result in a view similar to the following screenshot after a few hours of sensor measurements. Here, I can access the Pi using the external IP address outside my home network as I have added the HTTP port of 80 to the port forwarding settings of my home router.

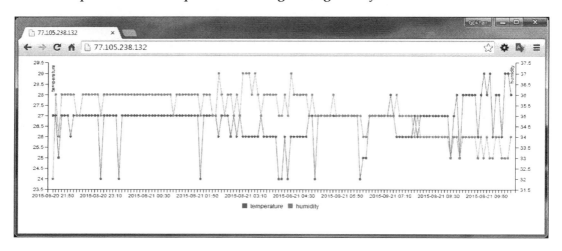

Now, we have a running FTP, database, and web servers. Let's administer these using ConnectBot.

Simple management of servers

The following command simply checks the status of the FTP server:

```
service vsftpd status
```

This command restarts the FTP server if there's any problem with it:

```
sudo service vstfpd restart
```

The `service` utility that we have used lets you restart the database and web server using these two commands:

```
sudo service mysql restart
sudo service apache2 restart
```

Use the following command to check the status of the MySQL server:

```
mysqladmin -u root -p status
```

If you believe that the database has grown too much in size, you can start the MySQL console and run a SQL query to see the database size:

```
mysql -u root -p
mysql> SELECT table_schema "DB", Round(Sum(data_length +
index_length) / 1024 / 1024, 1) "Size in MB"
FROM    information_schema.tables
GROUP  BY table_schema;
```

You can even delete records that are older than three days using the following query:

```
select measurements;
delete from measurements where ttime < NOW() - INTERVAL 3 DAY;
```

Or, as an alternative, you can check the size of the filesystem using the shell command:

```
df -h
```

Summary

This chapter introduced you to the management of Raspberry Pi as a server and how to issue commands to it from Android. We installed an FTP server on the Pi and shared files between Android clients. To show an example of database and web servers, we implemented a useful project and learned to manage these servers remotely as well.

The next chapter will introduce you to the Pi camera and help you implement a surveillance solution.

3

Live Streaming of a Surveillance Camera from the Pi

In this chapter, we will connect a camera to Raspberry Pi and stream a live video from it. We will then be able to watch the streaming of this content from our Android device. This chapter will move us closer to usage and away from administration of Raspberry Pi.

In this chapter, we will cover the following topics:

- Hardware and software configurations
- Streaming video to an Android device
- The surveillance mode

Hardware and software configurations

We will use a standard camera developed for the Pi that costs about $30 in many major electronics stores.

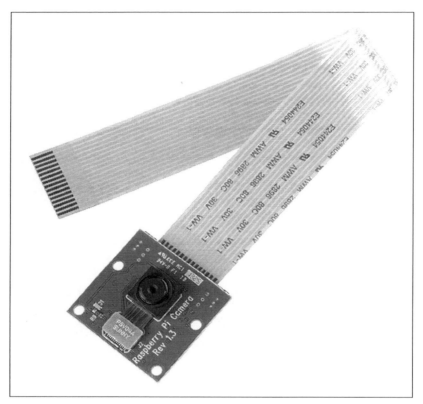

The Pi camera

Pi has a camera port where you can plug in the camera cable. The plug on the Pi can be opened by pulling it upwards. If you have problems connecting the camera to the Pi, you can find many videos on the Internet showing how to do it. You can watch one from Raspberry Pi Foundation at `https://www.raspberrypi.org/help/camera-module-setup/`.

The next step is to configure the Pi and enable the camera hardware. This is done using the Pi configuration program accessed by issuing the following command:

```
sudo raspi-config
```

In the menu provided, select **Enable Camera** and hit *Enter*. Then click on **Finish** where you'll be prompted to reboot.

Streaming video to an Android device

The easiest way to stream from the Pi to Android is using the **RaspiCam Remote** app that logs in to the Pi and executes the necessary commands. It then automatically gets the stream from the Pi. Download and open the app, where you will get an initial view to provide login details, such as the IP address, username, and password. Note that by default, it uses the default login account details and SSH port. You will only need the IP address if you have the default installation in place. You can even access your camera from the Internet if you enable port forwarding for port 22, as described in *Chapter 1, Make a Remote Desktop Connection to Your Pi from Anywhere*. The following screenshot displays the login settings of the RaspiCam Remote app:

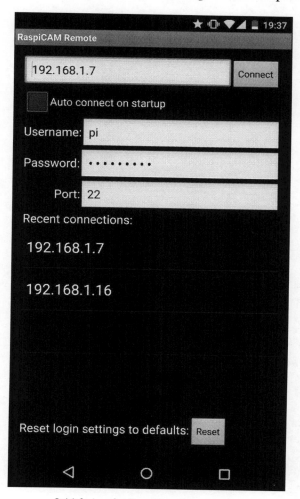

Initial view for RaspiCam Remote app

After waiting a few seconds, you should see the first picture taken by the Raspberry Pi camera on your Android device. On pressing the camera icon, the camera will start streaming as shown in the following screenshot:

Streaming from Pi

The next step is to get better streaming quality using the **H.264** setting. After connecting to the RaspiCam Remote app, you should open settings and check the **H.264** checkbox. However, before connecting through the app again, we need to install a VLC server on the Pi using the following command. You may experience problems with the `install` commands from time to time, but running it once again almost always solves the problem:

```
sudo apt-get install vlc
```

The next step is to install a better VLC client on the Android. We will use the **VLC for Android beta** app. After installing it, open RaspiCam Remote app again, and then start streaming by clicking on the camera icon. At this point, Android will ask you to select the standard video player or the newly installed VLC for Android beta. Choose the latter and you will experience a much better streaming quality. Do not forget to add port 8080 to the port forwarding settings on your router to get access to the streaming video over the Internet.

Manual VLC configurations

The RaspiCam Remote app automatically configures VLC on the Pi before it streams video content. Some of you might want to connect to the video stream directly from the VLC app and skip RaspiCam on Android. The following command is the same as the one that RaspiCam issues from the account that you provide before you start streaming using RaspiCam on your Android device:

```
/opt/vc/bin/raspivid -o - -n -t 0 -fps 25 -rot 0 -w 640 -h 480 |
/usr/bin/vlc -I dummy stream:///dev/stdin --sout
'#standard{access=http,mux=ts,dst=:8080}' :demux=h264 &
```

If you issue the preceding command, you will be able to view the streaming content from the VLC app. You can initiate a connection by clicking on the antenna-like icon on the action bar of the VLC app. It will prompt for the stream address, which is http://PI_IP_ADDRESS:8080.

The surveillance mode

It is cool to see the streaming from your camera, but it is much more useful to be able to run it in surveillance mode. We want the camera to react to motion and save images or videos whenever motion is detected, so that we can check them later instead of keeping an eye on the video. For this purpose, we will begin installing a motion recognition software on our Pi, which is called for apparent reasons, motion:

```
sudo apt-get install motion
```

This will install the motion software and the following command will add the necessary packages to the kernel:

```
sudo modprobe bcm2835-v4l2
```

It is a good idea to put this in the /etc/rc.local file so that it can be run at startup. You should put it before the exit 0 line, though.

We will even make some configuration changes to be able to access the streaming and control features that `motion` provides. Edit the configuration file of motion using the following command:

```
sudo nano /etc/motion/motion.conf
```

By default, the web access to motion is restricted to the localhost, which means that you cannot access it from another computer other than the Pi itself. We will change this behavior by finding the following lines in the `motion.conf` file:

```
webcam_localhost on
control_localhost on
```

Note that these are not consequent lines in the file. Also, if you use **nano** as your editor, you can press *Ctrl+W* to put it into the search mode.

We will turn off the localhost-only access behavior by replacing the preceding lines of code with the following ones, respectively:

```
webcam_localhost off
control_localhost off
```

In addition, we want the `motion` service to execute in the background mode as well being run as `daemon`. For this purpose, we should locate the following line of code in the same file:

```
daemon on
```

We should replace it with this line:

```
daemon off
```

If we start `motion` now, we will get the following error:

```
Exit motion, cannot create process id file (pid file)
/var/run/motion/motion.pid: No such file or directory
```

To get rid of this error, we can create this folder that `motion` is complaining about:

```
sudo mkdir /var/run/motion
```

Note that this directory might get deleted at startup, so it is a good idea to add this command in the `/etc/rc.local` file as well.

Now, you can finally start and stop your Pi camera in the surveillance mode, issuing the following commands, preferably using the **ConnectBot** app or any other SSH client that we discussed in the previous chapter. The following command will start `motion`:

```
sudo motion
```

To stop motion, issue the following command:

```
sudo pkill -f motion
```

If you always want to run it on startup, which I would not recommend as you can run out of storage space on your Pi, you should edit the `/etc/default/motion` file using the following command:

```
sudo nano /etc/default/motion
```

In this file, you will find the following line:

```
start_motion_daemon=no
```

You should replace it with this one:

```
start_motion_daemon=yes
```

You may either use the following command to start the service or reboot your Pi, which will start the service automatically:

```
sudo service motion start
```

To check the status of all the services as well as the motion service, you can use the following command:

```
sudo service --status-all
```

Motion software comes in two parts. The first part is where you can watch streaming videos, and the second part is where you can see image/video files when motion is detected. You can see the stream from the motion software by opening the `http://IP_ADRESS_OF_THE_PI:8081` web page. For some reason, this part of the motion software only works in Firefox, but the surveillance part discussed in the next section will work with other browsers. Note that you cannot start both the motion server and VLC through the RaspiCam app at the same time as they use the same port. The following screenshot shows the streaming of a motion video:

A motion streaming video on port 8081

You can log on to Pi using **AndFTP** as discussed in the previous chapter and navigate to the `/tmp/motion` folder to see images saved whenever motion is detected. Restarting the motion service will empty the contents of the folder.

 Add ports `8080`, `8081`, and FTP port `21` to your port forwarding settings inside your router to access these services from outside your network.

Accessing surveillance images on the Web

In almost all scenarios where surveillance is involved, we want to access saved images from when motion was detected through the Internet. To do this, we will connect the directory to which `motion` saves images to the Apache Server we have already installed in the previous chapter. Running the following command will do this trick:

```
sudo ln -s /tmp/motion /var/www/motion
```

You should also add this directory to which `motion` saves images and videos into the `motion.conf` file using the following line in the file:

```
target_dir /tmp/motion
```

Now, open the `http://IP_ADRESS_OF_THE_PI/motion` link in a browser and you will see the image listing that `motion` has saved whenever motion is detected in front of the camera.

Note that you may get an access forbidden fault from the web browser if `motion` has not yet detected any motion and created the `/tmp/motion/` directory. The following screenshot illustrates the image listing that motion has saved:

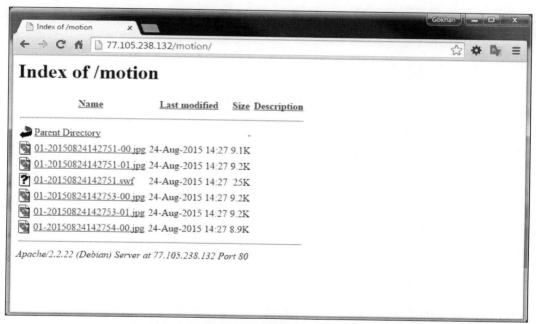

Image and video files when motion detected accessed through the Web

Summary

We have moved away from administration of Pi to more real-life projects and installed a camera on the Pi; thereby, viewing streams from the Pi on both an Android device and the Web. We have even learned how to use the Pi as a surveillance camera and see motion detected by it.

We will continue using the Pi in an even more interesting scenario in the next chapter and turn it into a media center.

4
Turn Your Pi into a Media Center

We have been administering our Pi and implementing useful projects in the previous chapters. In this chapter, we will use our Pi more as a source of entertainment and turn it into a media center. The topics covered are as follows:

- Installing and setting up a media center on the Pi
- Connecting to a media center via remote control from Android
- Getting more from your media center
- Installing a media center using NOOBS

Installing and setting up a media center on Pi

The media center software we've chosen for the purpose of this project is **Kodi**, formerly known as XBMC. It is open source and widely used with lots of add-ons.

As usual, we will start by installing the necessary software on our Pi using the `apt-get` command:

```
sudo apt-get install kodi
```

Then, we'll run the `kodi-standalone` executable, which will start Kodi and show its user interface on the HDMI port of the Pi. It is, therefore, important that you connect the Pi to a screen using the HDMI port instead of a remote desktop to see Kodi's user interface. Now, you can connect a USB keyboard or mouse to navigate inside Kodi.

Starting Kodi on boot

We definitely do not want to run a command to start the media center, no matter how easy it is to run commands from Android, as discussed in previous chapters. For this reason, we need to start the command on startup using the `crontab -e` command. Add the following line at the end of the file the `crontab` command command opens:

```
@reboot /usr/bin/kodi-standalone &
```

Now, whenever you restart the Pi, Kodi will be restarted automatically. Note that, here, you access the media center through the HDMI port of the Pi, but you will also be able to access via remote desktop using the tools discussed in *Chapter 1, Make a Remote Desktop Connection to Your Pi from Anywhere*.

Connecting to the media center via remote control from Android

The main problem with the current setup is that you can only control the media center using a connected keyboard or mouse, making it not as comfortable to use as a media center should be. However, there is a remote control for Kodi on Android, called **Kore**, that makes it really easy to remotely control the media center. You can download it from Google Play. Its official name is **Kore, Official Remote for Kodi** and it is published by the **XBMC Foundation**, which is a nonprofit organization that operates the Kodi Media Center project.

Before you can connect the remote control application on Android to the Kodi installation on the Pi, you need to make some setup changes on Kodi. Go to the **SYSTEM** menu in Kodi, and then **Settings**, **Services**, and **Webserver**. Here, you should select **Allow control of Kodi via HTTP**. Then go to the **Remote control** settings in same menu and enable the **Allow programs on this system to control XBMC** and **Allow programs on other systems to control XBMC** settings. Now open Kore on Android and let it search for the media center. If both the phone and media center are on the same network, Kore should be able to find it. When succeeded with the search, you will see a view similar to the following screenshot:

Note that the default HTTP port for Kodi collides with the motion server's default HTTP port, which we saw in the previous chapter. You should either change the port setting in Kodi or stop the motion server before making these changes in Kodi's settings.

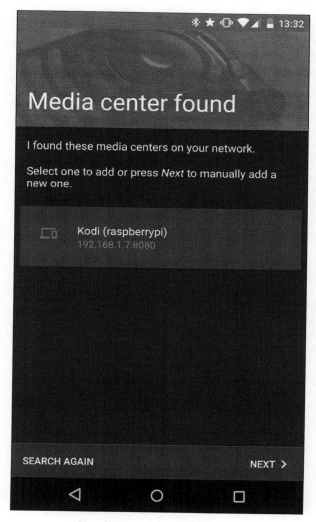

Kore has found the media center

Now, click on the newly found media center to connect and start controlling it remotely. If it does not identify the media center automatically, you can press the **Next** button and enter the parameters manually. Port 8080 is the default port and kodi is the default username you should use if you haven't changed these parameters inside Kodi.

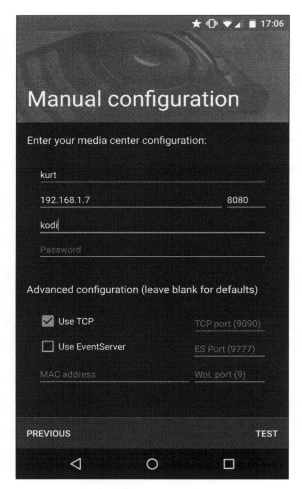

Manual settings in Kore

Getting more from your media center

There are many things a media center can be used for. You can, for example, download add-ons that give you access to lots of online content, such as YouTube, Khan Academy, and TED Talks.

Watching videos using Kodi on an Android device

Another interesting thing you can do is to upload video from your phone to the Pi using the previously discussed AndFTP app from *Chapter 2, Server Management with Pi*, and then watch movies using the media center. You need to add a directory on to the Pi where you will upload these files as a media location in Kodi. Go to **Videos | Files | Files**, and then navigate to **Add Videos....** Here, you should first select **Browse**, and then **Root filesystem**. Note that we were using /home/pi as the target for uploads in *Chapter 2, Server Management with Pi*. It should work even in this case. Browse down to this location and click on **OK** on all three pop ups. You should now see the Pi in the list of **Videos** on Kodi. You can even add this folder to favorites for easy access. Open the Kore remote control app and browse to the pi folder once again under **Videos**. When the pi folder is highlighted in Kodi, press the properties button in the Kore remote control app. Then select **Add to favorites** by scrolling down using the arrows on Kore.

The button that lists the choices in Kore, that is, the properties button

Next open AndFTP from *Chapter 2, Server Management with Pi*, and connect to the Pi or select the connection that is already saved from previous sessions. You should now see the contents of the /home/pi directory, which is the default location for the user pi we have used. This is the target location. Then, select the mobile phone image on the action bar in AndFTP to select a video located on your mobile phone and upload it to Kodi.

The AndFTP interface to select the upload location from the phone to the Pi

Recorded videos are generally located under DCIM/Camera. Select the videos you want to upload. Then, click on the upload icon in the action bar:

The AndFTP interface to begin upload from the phone to the Pi

Next, you can browse down to the pi directory in Kodi that we have added to the **Videos** section and see the videos you have just uploaded on your media center.

Streaming the Android display to Kodi

Another very interesting thing you can do is to stream your Android screen and make Kodi show this stream. For this purpose, we will first download an app from Google Play that will stream an Android display and publish it using a URL on your internal network. The app we will use for this purpose is called **Screen Stream Mirroring** and comes both as a free and a paid version. For the sake of this project, it is enough to download the free version. After starting the app, you will need to close a few advertisements and press the **Start Now** button on the pop-up.

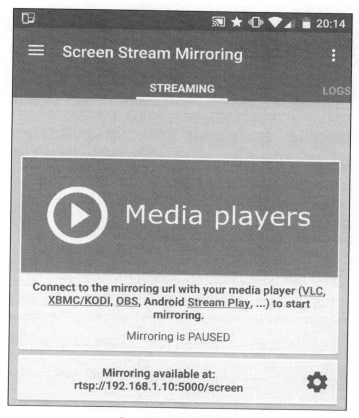

Screen Stream Mirroring

Here, you will see the address that the streaming is published to. We will now save this `rtsp://YOUR_ANDROID_IP_ADRESS:5000/screen` link in a file we will call `stream.strm` on the Pi under the `home` directory of the user `pi`, which is `/home/pi`. Then, browse to the `pi` directory in Kodi, find this file, and open it. Remember that we have saved this directory under the **Videos** section in Kodi and as a favorite as well. Now, you should be able to see whatever you do on the Android device's screen attached to the Pi's HDMI port used by Kodi. Another option here is to show the Android camera capture through this channel. The Screen Stream Mirroring app we use has a notification in the Android notification area. If you expand it, you will see an option named **CAMERA**. By pressing this button, you will be able to start the camera and see the camera capture as well.

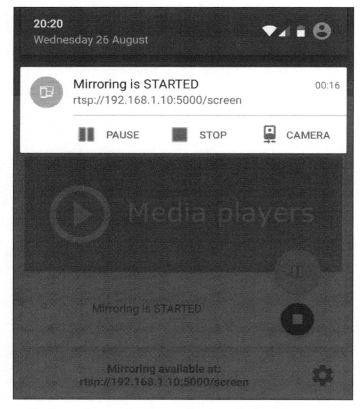

The Screen Stream Mirroring notification with the camera option

Installing the media center using NOOBS

Another option for installing the media center onto the Pi is using NOOBS. This way, users can very easily install the media center without worrying about details related to Raspbian OS, as we did in this chapter. We have already covered the NOOBS installation in *Chapter 1, Make a Remote Desktop Connection to Your Pi from Anywhere*. However, in *Chapter 1, Make a Remote Desktop Connection to Your Pi from Anywhere*, we used the offline installation option. We can use the online installation option instead. You should download the online NOOBS installer from `http://downloads.raspberrypi.org/NOOBS_lite_latest`. This ZIP file is much smaller but you need to connect the Pi to an Ethernet network before you begin installation. Extract the contents of the file to an SD card and restart your Pi with this SD card inserted. Now, you will see a list of operating systems to install. The list contains two media centers as well. These are **OpenELEC** and **OSMC**. Both are based on Kodi, which we've already covered in this chapter.

Summary

This chapter was short, but fun. We have learned to install on our Pi and set up one of the most widely used media centers and control it remotely from our Android device.

In the next chapter, we will get our hands dirty and begin some Python and Android programming, and make use of even more connection possibilities between the Pi and Android.

5

Missed Calls with Pi

In this chapter, we will implement a much more programming-oriented project and dive into Bluetooth Smart or **Bluetooth Low Energy (BLE)** programming. We will make the Pi and Android phones communicate through Bluetooth, and control the Pi using this channel. We will cover the following topics in this chapter:

- Installing the necessary components
- Adding a sensor service to Bluetooth Low Energy
- Connecting from an Android app
- Sending the reboot command from your Android phone to the Pi
- Sending more commands from your Android phone to the Pi

Installing the necessary components

The hardware component needed for this project is a BLE-enabled Bluetooth USB dongle. It is important that this hardware supports BLE as we will specifically make use of this part of the Bluetooth stack. We will use one by **Plugable**, which is available on Amazon.

The Bluetooth dongle by Plugable

The Raspbian distribution that we have downloaded already contains support for Bluetooth, but we need to update Bluetooth packages for better LE support. You can build and install a more modern of the Bluetooth package version using the following commands:

```
sudo apt-get install libdbus-1-dev libdbus-glib-1-dev libglib2.0-dev
libical-dev libreadline-dev libudev-dev libusb-dev make

mkdir -p work/bluepy

cd work/bluepy

wget https://www.kernel.org/pub/linux/bluetooth/bluez-5.33.tar.xz

tar xvf bluez-5.33.tar.xz

cd bluez-5.33

./configure --disable-systemd

make

sudo make install
```

The `make` step will compile the necessary packages needed for the Pi and will take about 15 minutes to complete. However, you'll need to be patient as it will lead to something cool and useful at the end. Note that the latest version of BlueZ is 5.33 at the time of writing this book, and you can instead replace it with the latest version by checking the list of all available versions at `https://www.kernel.org/pub/linux/bluetooth/`. Note here that we have disabled the `systemd` support using the `--disable-systemd` option, which causes build errors, otherwise.

The preceding commands have also installed some command-line tools to let us configure and scan for Bluetooth devices. The following command lists all the attached components on the USB ports of the Pi:

```
lsusb
```

The output of the preceding command is as follows:

```
Bus 001 Device 002: ID 0424:9514 Standard Microsystems Corp.

Bus 001 Device 001: ID 1d6b:0002 Linux Foundation 2.0 root hub

Bus 001 Device 003: ID 0424:ec00 Standard Microsystems Corp.

Bus 001 Device 004: ID 0a5c:21e8 Broadcom Corp.

Bus 001 Device 005: ID 148f:5370 Ralink Technology, Corp. RT5370
Wireless Adapter
```

The Bluetooth adapter is named `Broadcom` in my case. To get more details on a specific device, use the following command:

```
sudo lsusb -v -d 0a5c:
```

Here, note that `0a5c` is the first part of the address of the Bluetooth dongle that I am reusing to get more information on only this device.

The `hciconfig` tool will show you which devices support Bluetooth. This command outputs the following information on my system:

```
hci0:    Type: BR/EDR   Bus: USB
         BD Address: 5C:F3:70:68:BE:42   ACL MTU: 1021:8   SCO MTU: 64:1
         DOWN
         RX bytes:564 acl:0 sco:0 events:29 errors:0
         TX bytes:358 acl:0 sco:0 commands:29 errors:0
```

As seen here, the device is marked as DOWN. We will keep it this way as the next tool we install requires it to be down initially.

There are useful Bluetooth LE commands that you can use to check for other BLE devices. We will not use these commands yet, but it is a good practice to play with them to check if your BLE devices are working or accessible.

The same `hciconfig` tool that we've used previously helps us bring the Bluetooth device up. However, do not do this if you want to proceed with the rest of the chapter as the next tool requires it to be down:

```
sudo hciconfig hci0 up
```

It is a good idea to put this command in crontab, as discussed previously, using crontab with the -e option in order to let you use nano as the editor and install new crontab automatically. Add `@reboot sudo hciconfig hci0 up` inside the file at the end, and save and exit.

There are two other commands we can use:

```
sudo hcitool lescan
```

This command lists the BLE devices. Now let's take a look at the following command:

```
sudo hcitool lecc 68:64:4B:0B:24:A7
```

And this command tests the Bluetooth connection to the device. Note that the address provided to the latter command was returned by the former.

We will even need a programming support for Bluetooth. We will use **Go** as the language and the **Gatt** package for Go that gives support for Bluetooth LE in the Go language. The **Generic Attribute Profile (Gatt)** is a general specification to send and receive small amounts of data, known as attributes, over a BLE link. Let's run the following commands to install the go language:

```
cd
git clone https://go.googlesource.com/go
cd go
git checkout go1.4.1
cd src
./all.bash
```

You might want to go and grab a cup of coffee here, as the last command will take about 40 minutes to complete. At the end of the output, you will see that the go installer asks you to add a binary directory to your path for easy access. The following commands can accomplish this:

```
PATH=$PATH:/home/pi/go/bin
export PATH
export GOROOT=/home/pi/go
export GOPATH=/home/pi/gopath
```

> It is a good idea to put these commands in the /etc/profile file in order to execute them for each session that you start in the future. Be sure to add them at the end of the file, though. Also, do not forget to actually execute them even though you have put them in the profile file if you want to continue without rebooting.

Then, use the following command to download the Gatt package source files:

```
go get github.com/paypal/gatt
```

Now we will start a simple BLE server using the following command:

```
cd /home/pi/gopath/src/github.com/paypal/gatt
go build examples/server.go
sudo ./server
```

After completing this chapter, you might want to put the server startup command inside `crontab` using the following command:

```
crontab -e
```

This way the BLE server will start each time you reboot the Pi. Add the following line at the end:

```
@reboot sudo
/home/pi/gopath/src/github.com/paypal/gatt/server
```

It is now time to find our Raspberry Pi, which behaves like a BLE device from Android. We will use the **BLE Scanner** app by **BluePixel Technologies** and is available on the Play Store. When you start it, you will see a list of BLE devices available around you along with their addresses. The address of the Bluetooth adapter on the Pi can be seen using the `hciconfig` command. The default implementation of the Gatt server names the device as **Gopher**. The following screenshot illustrates the BLE Scanner app, showing the Pi as a BLE device:

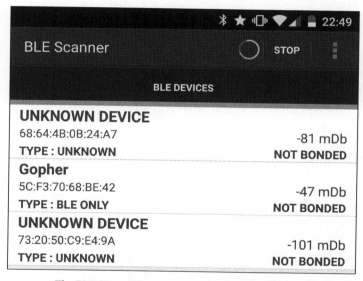

The BLE Scanner app showing the Pi as a BLE device

The BLE stack is designed in a way that a device supports some number of services that users can connect to, and each service can provide read/write or notification characteristics, which is mainly data that you can write to, read, or get notifications from. Click on the device in the app and you will connect to the Pi's newly started BLE server. You will be presented with four services. The one we are interested in is called **UNKNOWN SERVICE**, which is unnamed because it is not a standard service and it is implemented to only demonstrate the Gatt example server. Click on this service and you will see three characteristics provided by this service: **READ**, **WRITE**, and **Notification**. You can recognize the type of characteristic by looking at which one of the three buttons on BLE Scanner app is enabled. The following screenshot illustrates the READ characteristics:

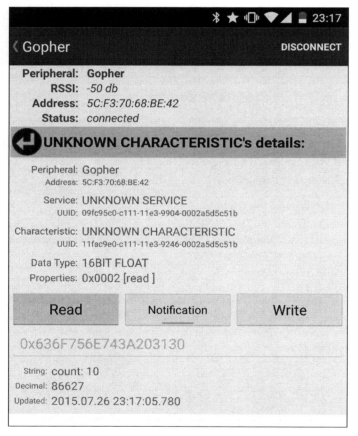

The READ characteristic

Adding a sensor service to Bluetooth Low Energy

We will add a new service to the already existing example from Gatt. This new service will publish two new characteristics to begin with: one for humidity and the other for temperature measurements. We will read the measurements the same way using the techniques we've discussed in *Chapter 2, Server Management with Pi.* To read these measurements, we will create two new files with content similar to the sense. py file that we discussed *Chapter 2, Server Management with Pi.* Let's create two files under the home directory, and name them humidity.py and temperature.py. The temperature.py file has the following content:

```python
#!/usr/bin/python

import sys
import Adafruit_DHT

humidity, temperature = Adafruit_DHT.read_retry(Adafruit_DHT.DHT11, 4)
print str(temperature)
```

The humidity.py file has similar content. The only difference is that it prints out the humidity part of the measurement instead of the temperature:

```python
#!/usr/bin/python

import sys
import Adafruit_DHT

humidity, temperature = Adafruit_DHT.read_retry(Adafruit_DHT.DHT11, 4)
print str(humidity)
```

We need to change the file access mode to executable as well using the following command:

```
chmod +x temperature.py humidity.py
```

Now, you can test sensor measurements using the following commands:

```
sudo ./temperature.py
sudo ./humidity.py
```

The next step is to publish these readings via the Bluetooth channel. We will create a new service inside the existing Gatt server example. For this purpose, you can start editing the server.go source file for the server example in the /home/pi/gopath/ src/github.com/paypal/gatt/examples path. You only need to add three lines of code in the function definition for onStateChanged in between other service definitions. In the following content, note that the count service and battery service already exist. We only need to add the sensor service:

```
// A simple count service for demo.
s1 := service.NewCountService()
d.AddService(s1)

// A sensor service for demo.
sSensor := service.NewSensorService()
d.AddService(sSensor)

// A fake battery service for demo.
s2 := service.NewBatteryService()
d.AddService(s2)
```

Additionally, in the same file, change the line where new services are advertised to the following code in order to advertise the new service as well:

```
// Advertise device name and service's UUIDs.
d.AdvertiseNameAndServices("Gopher", []gatt.UUID{s1.UUID(),
sSensor.UUID(), s2.UUID()})
```

We need to add the definition for the new service also. The following code should be placed in a file, named sensor.go, under the service directory of the Gatt examples at the same level as other service definition files, such as count.go and battery.go:

```
package service

import (
 "fmt"
 "log"
 "os/exec"
 "strings"

 "github.com/paypal/gatt"
)

func NewSensorService() *gatt.Service {
 s := gatt.NewService(gatt.MustParseUUID("19fc95c0-c111-11e3-9904-
0002a5d5c51b"))
```

```
  s.AddCharacteristic(gatt.MustParseUUID("21fac9e0-c111-11e3-9246-
0002a5d5c51b")).HandleReadFunc(
   func(rsp gatt.ResponseWriter, req *gatt.ReadRequest) {
    out, err := exec.Command("sh", "-c", "sudo
/home/pi/temperature.py").Output()
     if err != nil {
      fmt.Fprintf(rsp, "error occured %s", err)
      log.Println("Wrote: error %s", err)
     } else {
      stringout := string(out)
      stringout = strings.TrimSpace(stringout)
      fmt.Fprintf(rsp, stringout)
      log.Println("Wrote:", stringout)
     }
  })

  s.AddCharacteristic(gatt.MustParseUUID("31fac9e0-c111-11e3-9246-
0002a5d5c51b")).HandleReadFunc(
   func(rsp gatt.ResponseWriter, req *gatt.ReadRequest) {
    out, err := exec.Command("sh", "-c", "sudo
/home/pi/humidity.py").Output()
     if err != nil {
      fmt.Fprintf(rsp, "error occured %s", err)
      log.Println("Wrote: error %s", err)
     } else {
      stringout := string(out)
      stringout = strings.TrimSpace(stringout)
      fmt.Fprintf(rsp, stringout)
      log.Println("Wrote:", stringout)
     }
  })

  return s
 }
```

We need to build and rerun our server code using go. The following commands that we used earlier will help us do this. Note that you should be in the /home/pi/ gopath/src/github.com/paypal/gatt directory:

```
go build examples/server.go
sudo ./server
```

We can use the BLE Scanner app on Android again to connect to this new service and read the temperature and humidity sensor values. The following screenshot illustrates the Gopher services:

After connecting to the Gopher device, you should see the newly added service with the `19fc95c0-c111-11e3-9904-0002a5d5c51b` ID, and new characteristics for that service as shown in the following screenshot:

Newly added characteristics: one for temperature and the other for humidity measurements

The following screenshot illustrates the characteristic details for temperature measurement after pressing the the **Read** button:

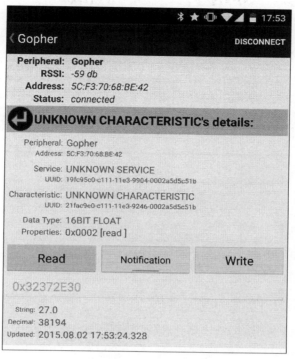

Characteristics for temperature measurement showing a current value of 27 degrees

Connecting from an Android app

We have used an existing app to connect to the BLE service that we implemented on Raspberry Pi. This app, called BLE Scanner, is very general purpose and would work for any kind of BLE device. However, we need a more specialized app that only reads measurements and abstracts away details of the BLE protocol, such as device scan, services, and service characteristics. In this section, we will implement an Android app to connect to the Raspberry Pi BLE. We need to install the Android Studio for this purpose. Android studio is specifically designed for Android app development by Google. You can read more about it by visiting `http://developer.android.com/tools/studio/`. You can find instructions for installation at `http://developer.android.com/sdk/`. We will use a real device to test our app and not the built-in emulator. For this purpose, you may need to install device drivers specific to your Android phone and make configuration changes to the Android Studio installation. The `http://developer.android.com/tools/device.html` link will help you carry out these actions.

Now, start the Android Studio and choose a new project to create. I will name the application `BLEPi` and the domain `example.com`. You should choose **Phone and Tablet** as the form factor, and at least **Android 5.0** as the minimum SDK as better BLE support is introduced with this SDK to the Android system. The core BLE support is actually added to Android 4.3, and the code files distributed on the book's website as well as the GitHub repository of the book will work for Android 4.3 as well as Android 5.0. However, for the sake of simplicity and ease, the upcoming code is for Android 5.0 only. Note that you should have downloaded Android 5.0 SDK during the Android Studio installation in order to be able to choose it in the create project wizard. Take a look at the links we've just mentioned in this section for further details on this. Then, choose to add a blank activity to the app and do not change the name of the activity in the next step; we will keep it as `MainActivity`.

We will begin our implementation by adding Bluetooth permissions to the `AndroidManifest.xml` file inside the `manifest` and before the `application` tag:

```
<uses-permission
android:name="android.permission.BLUETOOTH"/>
<uses-permission
android:name="android.permission.BLUETOOTH_ADMIN"/>
```

Then, we'll begin making changes to the `MainActivity.java` file. Start by making the following class variable definitions:

```
private BluetoothAdapter bluetoothAdapter;
private BluetoothLeScanner bleScanner;
private BluetoothGatt bleGatt;
private static final int REQUEST_ENABLE_BT = 1;
private static final UUID UUID_Service =
UUID.fromString("19fc95c0-c111-11e3-9904-0002a5d5c51b");
private static final UUID UUID_TEMPERATURE =
UUID.fromString("21fac9e0-c111-11e3-9246-0002a5d5c51b");
private static final UUID UUID_HUMIDITY =
UUID.fromString("31fac9e0-c111-11e3-9246-0002a5d5c51b");
```

The `bluetoothAdapter` definition represents the local device's Bluetooth adapter and lets you perform fundamental Bluetooth tasks, such as discovering other devices and getting the properties of the discovered devices. `bleScanner` provides methods to perform scan-related operations specific to Bluetooth LE devices and `bleGatt` provides the Bluetooth GATT functionality to enable communication with Bluetooth Smart devices. The UUIDs we have defined here are the same as the ones we have used in the `sensor.go` file that we saved on the Pi previously for the identification of the new service and its two new characteristics.

In the Android Studio, you can use the *Alt+Enter* shortcut key to automatically import missing packages. The cursor should be located on the class for which the import is missing in the java file. Or, alternatively, place the cursor on the class, keep the mouse pointer on it, and you will see a light bulb menu. In this menu, you can select the import class option.

Inside the onCreate method, which is called by the Android system when the app starts for the first time, we can initialize bluetoothAdapter:

```
BluetoothManager bluetoothManager =
(BluetoothManager) getSystemService(Context.BLUETOOTH_SERVICE);
bluetoothAdapter = bluetoothManager.getAdapter();
```

We need to define the startScan method that will be called whenever we want to initiate a scan of BLE devices.

```
private void startScan() {
    if (bluetoothAdapter == null || !bluetoothAdapter.isEnabled())
    {
    Intent enableBtIntent =
        new Intent(BluetoothAdapter.ACTION_REQUEST_ENABLE);
    startActivityForResult(enableBtIntent, REQUEST_ENABLE_BT);
    } else {
    bleScanner = bluetoothAdapter.getBluetoothLeScanner();
        if (bleScanner != null) {
            final ScanFilter scanFilter =
                new ScanFilter.Builder().build();
        ScanSettings settings =
            new ScanSettings.Builder()
                .setScanMode(ScanSettings.SCAN_MODE_LOW_LATENCY)
                .build();
        bleScanner.startScan(
            Arrays.asList(scanFilter), settings, scanCallback);
    }
    }
}
```

Here, we check if Bluetooth is enabled on the device first. If not, we'll present a message box to let the user enable Bluetooth. If it is enabled, we'll get an instance of bleScanner, which is used to start a scan using the startScan method. We can give a callback implementation name, such as scanCallback, which will be called whenever a scan returns some results. Now, we need to define this callback variable, as shown in the following code:

```
private ScanCallback scanCallback = new ScanCallback() {
    @Override
    public void onScanResult(int callbackType, ScanResult result) {
        if("Gopher".equals(result.getDevice().getName())) {
            Toast.makeText(MainActivity.this, "Gopher found",
                Toast.LENGTH_SHORT).show();
            if(bleScanner != null) {
                bleScanner.stopScan(scanCallback);
            }
            bleGatt =
                result.getDevice().connectGatt(
                    getApplicationContext(), false, bleGattCallback);
        }
        super.onScanResult(callbackType, result);
    }
};
```

The ScanCallback implementation overrides one important method, onScanResult, which is called whenever there is any new device to report. We then check if the device name is the same as the one that was defined in the server.go file on the Pi. If so, we can save the device properties and connection information to the bleGatt variable. We can even connect to the device using the connectGatt method, and provide another callback implementation, bleGattCallback, which will be called whenever an Android system establishes a connection to the device. We stop the scan if we have found the device we are looking for. Here is the definition for this callback:

```
private BluetoothGattCallback bleGattCallback = new
BluetoothGattCallback() {
    @Override
    public void onConnectionStateChange(BluetoothGatt gatt, int
status, int newState) {
        gatt.discoverServices();
        super.onConnectionStateChange(gatt, status, newState);
    }

    @Override
```

```
    public void onServicesDiscovered(BluetoothGatt gatt, int
status) {
        BluetoothGattService service =
            gatt.getService(UUID_Service);
        BluetoothGattCharacteristic temperatureCharacteristic =
            service.getCharacteristic(UUID_TEMPERATURE);
        gatt.readCharacteristic(temperatureCharacteristic);
        super.onServicesDiscovered(gatt, status);
    }


    @Override
    public void onCharacteristicRead(BluetoothGatt gatt, final
BluetoothGattCharacteristic characteristic, int status) {
        final String value = characteristic.getStringValue(0);
        runOnUiThread(new Runnable() {
            @Override
            public void run() {
                TextView tv;
                if(UUID_HUMIDITY.equals(characteristic.getUuid())) {
                    tv = (TextView) MainActivity.this.findViewById(
                        R.id.humidity_textview);
                } else {
                    tv = (TextView) MainActivity.this.findViewById(
                        R.id.temperature_textview);
                 }
                 tv.setText(value);
            }
        });

        BluetoothGattService service =
            gatt.getService(UUID_Service);
        readNextCharacteristic(gatt, characteristic);
        super.onCharacteristicRead(gatt, characteristic, status);
    }
};
```

In this callback implementation, we override three important methods called from the Android system on different times. The `onConnectionStateChange` method is called whenever a connection is established to the remote device through Bluetooth. In this case, we can initiate the service discovery of the device using the `discoverServices` method. The `onServicesDiscovered` method is then called when services are discovered on the device. In such a case, we'll read, to begin with, the temperature characteristics for the sensor service that we've defined on the Pi using the `readCharacteristic` method. Whenever the value of the characteristic reading operation has succeeded the third overridden method, `onCharacteristicRead` is called where we read the next characteristic which is humidity, and then wait for this operation to succeed in the same method. Then, we take turns to read the humidity and temperature values using the `readNextCharacteristic` method that we'll define in the same callback implementation. This is because the BLE protocol does not let us read both characteristics at the same time. Let's take a look at the following code:

```
private void readNextCharacteristic(BluetoothGatt gatt,
BluetoothGattCharacteristic characteristic) {
    BluetoothGattService service = gatt.getService(UUID_Service);
    if (UUID_HUMIDITY.equals(characteristic.getUuid())) {
        BluetoothGattCharacteristic temperatureCharacteristic =
            service.getCharacteristic(UUID_TEMPERATURE);
        gatt.readCharacteristic(temperatureCharacteristic);
    } else {
        BluetoothGattCharacteristic humidityCharacteristic =
            service.getCharacteristic(UUID_HUMIDITY);
        gatt.readCharacteristic(humidityCharacteristic);
    }
}
```

Whenever the respective read operation succeeds, we get the value of the measurement using the `getStringValue` method of the returned `characteristic` object, and then show it in the UI elements that we will define in the `activity_main.xml` file as follows:

```
<TextView
        android:id="@+id/temperature_textview"
        android:layout_width="wrap_content"
        android:layout_height="wrap_content"
        android:layout_alignParentEnd="true" />

    <TextView
        android:id="@+id/humidity_textview"
        android:layout_width="wrap_content"
        android:layout_height="wrap_content" />
```

For the code to be complete, we need to define the following methods as well in the `MainActivity.java` file:

```java
@Override
protected void onActivityResult(int requestCode, int resultCode,
Intent data) {
    if(requestCode == REQUEST_ENABLE_BT) {
        startScan();
    }
    super.onActivityResult(requestCode, resultCode, data);
}


@Override
protected void onResume() {
    startScan();
    super.onResume();
}


@Override
protected void onPause() {
    if(bleScanner != null) {
        bleScanner.stopScan(scanCallback);
        }

    if (bleGatt != null) {
        bleGatt.close();
        bleGatt.disconnect();
        bleGatt = null;
    }
    super.onPause();
}
```

The `onActivityResult` method is called whenever a user enables Bluetooth, and we need to start scanning in this case as well as every time the user starts an app where `onResume` is called. If the user closes the app, the Bluetooth connection can be stopped through the `onPause` method.

This is a great opportunity to test our the first version of our app that we have implemented so far and verify that it works. Select **Run app** in the **Run** menu in the Android Studio, and you will be given an option to select the location to install the app. You will then see the Android device that you have attached to your computer in the list.

Sending the reboot command from your Android phone to the Pi

Until now, we have been receiving data from the Pi through BLE. Now, we will send commands to it using the same channel. We will implement a new write characteristic in the same service as our temperature and humidity read characteristics are, which were defined on the Pi. Using these new characteristics, we will send the reboot command to the Pi. Let's begin by editing the **sensor.go** file again and put the following code at the end of it:

```
s.AddCharacteristic(gatt.MustParseUUID("41fac9e0-c111-11e3-9246-
0002a5d5c51b")).HandleWriteFunc(
  func(r gatt.Request, data []byte) (status byte) {
  log.Println("Command received")
  exec.Command("sh", "-c", "sudo reboot").Output()
  return gatt.StatusSuccess
})
```

Build and restart the BLE server using the following commands:

```
cd /home/pi/gopath/src/github.com/paypal/gatt
go build examples/server.go
sudo ./server
```

Now, test the characteristics mentioned previously using the BLE Scanner app. Whenever you write something to these characteristics, the Pi will reboot.

The next step is to implement this new reboot function in the Android app that we have been building.

First, add the UUID of the this new write characteristics we have just defined and a variable to control the operation sequences, as shown in the following code:

```
private static final UUID UUID_REBOOT =
  UUID.fromString("41fac9e0-c111-11e3-9246-0002a5d5c51b");
private volatile boolean isSendReboot = false;
```

The boolean variable, `isSendReboot`, will be used to initiate the write characteristic operation and orchestrate it together with the read operations previously defined. The BLE stack cannot handle read/write operations that are too close to each other, and we want to avoid performing one operation before the previous one is completed. Then, in the `onCharacteristicRead` function of `bleGattCallback`, change the line where we call `readNextCharacteristic` with the following piece of code:

```
if(isSendReboot) {
    BluetoothGattCharacteristic rebootCharacteristic =
        service.getCharacteristic(UUID_REBOOT);
    rebootCharacteristic.setValue("reboot");
    gatt.writeCharacteristic(rebootCharacteristic);
} else {
    readNextCharacteristic(gatt, characteristic);
}
```

Here, we will write a value, `reboot`, to the reboot characteristic if the control variable is set, by clicking a button that we will soon implement. We can override another method in `bleGattCallback`:

```
@Override
public void onCharacteristicWrite(BluetoothGatt gatt,
BluetoothGattCharacteristic characteristic, int status) {
    isSendReboot = false;
    readNextCharacteristic(gatt, characteristic);
    super.onCharacteristicWrite(gatt, characteristic, status);
}
```

This method is called whenever the write characteristic operation succeeds when we reset our control variable and continue with the read operations. Those of you who are observant might see a minor problem with this code, namely that we are sending a reboot command to the Pi, but at the same time, we're also trying to read characteristics from the Bluetooth device located on the same device that we are trying to reboot. These readings will not work when the Pi reboots, and our app will not be able to reconnect if we do not close and reopen it after the reboot has been completed successfully. The solution to this issue will be left as an exercise for you.

The last part of the implementation is to add a button for the command to our user interface and connect this button to a method in the `MainAcitivity.java` file which will be executed whenever the button is pressed. Add the following lines to the `activity_main.xml` file inside the `RelativeLayout` tag to begin with:

```
<Button
        android:id="@+id/reboot_button"
        android:layout_width="wrap_content"
        android:layout_height="wrap_content"
        android:layout_below="@id/humidity_textview"
        android:text="Reboot"
        android:onClick="sendRebootCommand"
        android:enabled="false"/>
```

Define the `sendRebootCommand` method in the `MainActivity.java` file:

```
public void sendRebootCommand(View v) throws InterruptedException
{
isSendReboot = true;
}
```

The only thing this function does when the **Reboot** button is clicked on is set the control variable that we have defined previously.

You can also add the following code in the `onScanResult` method of the `ScanCallback` class instance after the call to the `device.connectGatt` method to enable the button when we connect to Raspberry Pi via Bluetooth:

```
if(bleGatt != null) {
    MainActivity.this.findViewById(R.id.reboot_button).setEnabled
(true);
}
```

This is a good place to test the app again and see if you can successfully restart the Pi through an Android device.

Sending more commands from your Android phone to the Pi

In the previous section, we have sent the reboot command from Android to the Pi. In this section, we will send two new commands. One to light up a LED that we will connect to the Pi, and another to play sound on the Pi. These commands will be reused in the forthcoming sections.

Lighting the LEDs

We'll begin by connecting a LED light to the GPIO ports of the Pi. The LEDs usually come with a short and long leg. Connect a resistor to the short leg of the LED, and connect a female/female jumper to the other side of the resistor. This jumper should then be connected to one of the ground pins of the Pi. Take a look at the schema in *Chapter 2, Server Management with Pi*, to identify the pins. Note that we already used one of the ground pins when we connected our temperature-humidity sensor to the Pi. However, there are plenty of ground pins available. The long leg of the LED should be connected to one of the GPIO pins. We will choose number 17. You can take a look the GPIO port mappings diagram in *Chapter 2, Server Management with Pi*, to identify port 17.

[It is a good idea to choose a resistor in the span of 270Ω to 470Ω. This resistor to protects the LED lamp from unexpected voltage changes. If you choose a resistor with lower ohm values, then the LED will be brighter.]

We will access the GPIO and LED lamp using a software utility called **wiringPi**. We can download and install it using the following commands:

```
cd
git clone git://git.drogon.net/wiringPi
cd wiringPi
./build
```

These commands have helped us to install a command-line tool called `gpio`, which you can now use to light the LED lamp:

```
gpio -g mode 17 out
gpio -g write 17 1
```

You can turn it off using the following comand:

```
gpio -g write 17 0
```

We need to add two new characteristics to our BLE server implementation: the first to turn the light on, and the second to turn it off. Add the following lines to the end of the `sensor.go` file, and note that we have new UUIDs for each new characteristic that we create:

```
s.AddCharacteristic(gatt.MustParseUUID("51fac9e0-c111-11e3-9246-
0002a5d5c51b")).HandleWriteFunc(
  func(r gatt.Request, data []byte) (status byte) {
    log.Println("Command received to turn on")
    exec.Command("sh", "-c", "gpio -g mode 17 out").Output()
```

```
    exec.Command("sh", "-c", "gpio -g write 17 1").Output()
    return gatt.StatusSuccess
})

s.AddCharacteristic(gatt.MustParseUUID("61fac9e0-c111-11e3-9246-
0002a5d5c51b")).HandleWriteFunc(
  func(r gatt.Request, data []byte) (status byte) {
    log.Println("Command received to turn off")
    exec.Command("sh", "-c", "gpio -g mode 17 out").Output()
    exec.Command("sh", "-c", "gpio -g write 17 0").Output()
    return gatt.StatusSuccess
})
```

Now, build and restart the BLE server again. If you have added the BLE server command inside the crontab, you might need to reboot the Pi. Next, connect to the Pi using the BLE Scanner app again and use the **Write** button on characteristics section in the app to write values to these characteristics. You will need to provide some text to write to, otherwise, the BLE Scanner app will not send commands. Once you do this, you will be able to turn the LED on and off.

 It is always a good idea to check the new characteristics you've added in BLE Scanner app before you try to access it with the app that we are building. This way, we can be sure that we have added the characteristics correctly on the Pi side.

The next step is to implement this new function in our app. We can begin by introducing two new buttons in the `activity_main.xml` file:

```
<Button
        android:id="@+id/turnon_button"
        android:layout_width="wrap_content"
        android:layout_height="wrap_content"
        android:layout_below="@id/reboot_button"
        android:text="Turn on"
        android:onClick="sendTurnOnCommand"
        android:enabled="false"/>

    <Button
        android:id="@+id/turnoff_button"
        android:layout_width="wrap_content"
        android:layout_height="wrap_content"
        android:layout_below="@id/turnon_button"
        android:text="Turn off"
        android:onClick="sendTurnOffCommand"
        android:enabled="false"/>
```

In `MainActivity.java`, define the new UUID and control variables for the new characteristics:

```
private static final UUID UUID_TURNON =
    UUID.fromString("51fac9e0-c111-11e3-9246-0002a5d5c51b");
private static final UUID UUID_TURNOFF =
    UUID.fromString("61fac9e0-c111-11e3-9246-0002a5d5c51b");
private volatile boolean isSendTurnOn = false;
private volatile boolean isSendTurnOff = false;
```

In the `onScanResult` method of `scanCallback`, add the following code in the if-statement to enable these two buttons just after enabling the reboot button:

```
MainActivity.this.findViewById(R.id.turnon_button).setEnabled
(true);

MainActivity.this.findViewById(R.id.turnoff_button).setEnabled
(true);
```

In the `onCharacteristicRead` method of `bleGattCallback`, add new else-if statements to the existing check of the control variable for `isSendReboot`. The new code will look similar to the following:

```
if(isSendReboot) {
    BluetoothGattCharacteristic rebootCharacteristic =
        service.getCharacteristic(UUID_REBOOT);
    rebootCharacteristic.setValue("reboot");
    gatt.writeCharacteristic(rebootCharacteristic);
} else if(isSendTurnOn) {
    BluetoothGattCharacteristic turnOnCharacteristic =
        service.getCharacteristic(UUID_TURNON);
    turnOnCharacteristic.setValue("turnon");
    gatt.writeCharacteristic(turnOnCharacteristic);
} else if(isSendTurnOff) {
    BluetoothGattCharacteristic turnOffCharacteristic =
        service.getCharacteristic(UUID_TURNOFF);
    turnOffCharacteristic.setValue("turnoff");
    gatt.writeCharacteristic(turnOffCharacteristic);
} else {
    readNextCharacteristic(gatt, characteristic);
}
```

In the `onCharacteristicWrite` method, add the following code snippet to reset the control variables:

```
isSendTurnOn = false;
isSendTurnOff = false;
```

Finally, add new functions that can be called on click events for the new buttons:

```
public void sendTurnOnCommand(View v) throws InterruptedException
{
    isSendTurnOn = true;
}

public void sendTurnOffCommand(View v) throws InterruptedException
{
    isSendTurnOff = true;
}
```

Your app will look similar to the following screenshot:

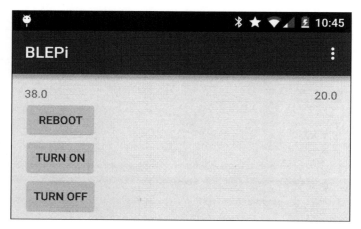

The final version of the app

Be patient to see the effects of the new buttons after clicking on them as it will take a few seconds for the messages to arrive in the Pi, and for the the LED lamp to be turned on.

Playing sounds on your Pi

To be able to play sounds on the Pi, sound modules should be loaded on reboot. To do this, we need to add sound module specifications to the `/etc/modules` file. Add `snd-bcm2835` in this file if it does not already exist there.

> You can use the `lsmod` command-line tool to see which modules are loaded at the moment:
>
> ```
> sudo modprobe snd_bcm2835
> ```
>
> This command loads the sound module without rebooting for the contents of the `/etc/modules` file to take effect.

We even need to find an audio file to play, which we can download using the following command:

```
cd
wget
http://www.freespecialeffects.co.uk/soundfx/sirens/whistle_blow_01.wa
v
```

You can now play this sound using the following command:

```
aplay whistle_blow_01.wav
```

> Note that that the audio channel might default due to HDMI output and you may not hear anything on your 3.5mm jack. In this case, you can run the following command to set the default audio player to the 3.5mm jack:
>
> ```
> amixer cset numid=3 1
> ```

The next step is to add the new write characteristic to the `sensor.go` file, as shown in the following code:

```
s.AddCharacteristic(gatt.MustParseUUID("71fac9e0-c111-11e3-9246-
0002a5d5c51b")).HandleWriteFunc(
  func(r gatt.Request, data []byte) (status byte) {
    log.Println("Command received to whistle ")
    exec.Command("sh", "-c", "aplay /home/pi/whistle_blow_01.wav").
Output()
    return gatt.StatusSuccess
  })
```

Do not forget to build and restart the Pi using the `go build examples/server.go` command. Next, define a new button in the `activity_main.xml` file:

```
<Button
        android:id="@+id/whistle_button"
        android:layout_width="wrap_content"
        android:layout_height="wrap_content"
        android:layout_below="@id/turnoff_button"
        android:text="Whistle"
        android:onClick="sendWhistleCommand"
        android:enabled="false"/>
```

Define a new event handler for the `onClick` event in the `MainActivity.java` file:

```
public void sendWhistleCommand(View v) throws InterruptedException
{
    isSendWhistle = true;
}
```

Next, add new the UUID and control variables to the same file:

```
private static final UUID UUID_WHISTLE =
    UUID.fromString("71fac9e0-c111-11e3-9246-0002a5d5c51b");
private volatile boolean isWhistle = false;
```

Enable the new button in the `onScanResult` method of the `scanCallback` instance variable inside the if-statement for the `bleGatt` null check:

```
MainActivity.this.findViewById(R.id.whistle_button).setEnabled
(true);
```

Add the following code in the new else-if statement in the `onCharacteristicRead` handler for the `bleGattCallback` variable:

```
else if(isSendWhistle) {
    BluetoothGattCharacteristic whistleCharacteristic =
        service.getCharacteristic(UUID_WHISTLE);
    whistleCharacteristic.setValue("whistle");
    gatt.writeCharacteristic(whistleCharacteristic);
}
```

Add a new statement to reset the control variable in the `onCharacteristicWrite` method:

```
isSendWhistle = false;
```

Now the whistle command is ready to be tested from our app.

Combining the commands and being informed on incoming calls

In this last section, we will combine the whistle and LED light up commands and initiate this new command whenever our phone rings. By now, we are used to creating new characteristics. Here is a new one to be added to `sensor.go` file:

```
s.AddCharacteristic(gatt.MustParseUUID("81fac9e0-c111-11e3-9246-
0002a5d5c51b")).HandleWriteFunc(
   func(r gatt.Request, data []byte) (status byte) {
   log.Println("Command received to turn on and whistle")
   exec.Command("sh", "-c", "aplay /home/pi/whistle_blow_01.wav").
Output()
   exec.Command("sh", "-c", "gpio -g mode 17 out").Output()
   exec.Command("sh", "-c", "gpio -g write 17 1").Output()
   return gatt.StatusSuccess
  })
```

We can combine these two commands to save ourselves from the development details of sending two separate commands as a single transaction. We need a new permission in the `AndroidManifest.xml` file to get an incoming call state from the Android system:

```
<uses-permission
android:name="android.permission.READ_PHONE_STATE" />
```

We also need new instance variables in `MainActivity.java`:

```
private static final UUID UUID_WHISTLE_AND_TURNON =
    UUID.fromString("81fac9e0-c111-11e3-9246-0002a5d5c51b");
private volatile boolean isSendWhistleAndTurnOn = false;
```

Then, we need to get an instance of a system phone service and attach our own listener to it. Add these two lines of code in the `onCreate` method:

```
TelephonyManager TelephonyMgr = (TelephonyManager)
    getSystemService(Context.TELEPHONY_SERVICE);
TelephonyMgr.listen(new PhoneListener(),
PhoneStateListener.LISTEN_CALL_STATE);
```

Next, define a local `PhoneListener` class:

```
class PhoneListener extends PhoneStateListener {
   public void onCallStateChanged(int state, String
incomingNumber) {
       super.onCallStateChanged(state, incomingNumber);
       switch (state) {
```

```
          case TelephonyManager.CALL_STATE_RINGING:
              Toast.makeText(getApplicationContext(), incomingNumber,
Toast.LENGTH_LONG).show();
              Toast.makeText(getApplicationContext(),
"CALL_STATE_RINGING", Toast.LENGTH_LONG).show();
              isSendWhistleAndTurnOn = true;
              break;
          default:
              break;
          }
      }
  }
```

Here, whenever we get a state change on the phone, we check if this is a CALL_STATE_RINGING state. If it is, we can set the control variable for the newly created command in the same way as the button click event handlers did for previously defined commands. Then, we can add this additional else-if statement in the onCharacteristic read method as well:

```
else if(isSendWhistleAndTurnOn) {
    BluetoothGattCharacteristic whistleAndTurnOnCharacteristic =
        service.getCharacteristic(UUID_WHISTLE_AND_TURNON);
    whistleAndTurnOnCharacteristic.setValue("whistleturnon");
    gatt.writeCharacteristic(whistleAndTurnOnCharacteristic);
}
```

Next, we'll reset the control variable in the onCharacteristicWrite method as follows:

```
isSendWhistleAndTurnOn = false;
```

Now, you will be able to see the LED lamp turned on and hear the whistle sound on the Pi as soon as your phone rings. Note that our app needs to be started and visible for this to work. This is caused by one of the two main issues with the code we have. All the communication with the Pi through BLE should actually be done in side an Android service, and phone events need to be handled inside BroadcastReceiver instead of in an **activity**. Both of these implementations, that is, Pi communication and phone state interception, should actually be separated from the **activity**. An activity should actually be a UI component and nothing more. However, our intention here was to show you only the fun parts and be quick and dirty. These further improvements on the Android code will be left as an exercise for you.

Summary

In this chapter, we covered a lot of content, ranging from BLE implementations on the Pi to details of the Android BLE code. We had great fun with the Pi and came up with a useful project that can be developed further.

In the next chapter, we will learn more ways to make use of BLE equipment on the Pi and use our phones not just as Android devices, but also as access points for the Pi.

6

The Vehicle Pi

We will continue to use Bluetooth on our Pi in this chapter to track the location and data from our car. The following sections will be covered in this chapter:

- Finding out the location of the car
- Using your Android device as an access point
- Collecting the car data
- Sending data to the cloud
- Putting it all together

Finding out the car location

In this chapter, we will collect the engine data from our car, but things will get more exciting if we can gather some for of location data as well. For this purpose, we will connect a USB GPS receiver to the Pi and receive our location through this piece of equipment. We will use one of the cheapest receivers available in the market, as shown in the following image:

The Globalsat BU-353 GPS receiver

After connecting the GPS to the Pi, you can issue the `lsusb` command to see if it is registered correctly. The output from this command on my system is as follows, and here `Prolific` is the GPS adapter:

```
Bus 001 Device 002: ID 0424:9514 Standard Microsystems Corp.

Bus 001 Device 001: ID 1d6b:0002 Linux Foundation 2.0 root hub

Bus 001 Device 003: ID 0424:ec00 Standard Microsystems Corp.

Bus 001 Device 004: ID 148f:5370 Ralink Technology, Corp. RT5370
Wireless Adapter

Bus 001 Device 005: ID 067b:2303 Prolific Technology, Inc. PL2303
Serial Port

Bus 001 Device 006: ID 0a5c:21e8 Broadcom Corp.
```

The next thing we need to install is a GPS daemon that receives location information from the adapter:

```
sudo apt-get install gpsd gpsd-clients python-gps
```

You might need to reboot in order to get the daemon to start. Otherwise, you can issue the following command to get it working immediately:

```
sudo gpsd /dev/ttyUSB0 -F /var/run/gpsd.sock
```

The installation script has even provided us with a tool to see the current GPS location and the satellites that are in range through a text-based window:

```
cgps -s
```

 The GPS receiver works best outdoors or with a clear view of the sky near a window.

The output on my system and in my location from the `cgps` command is shown in the following screenshot:

```
lqqqqqqqqqqqqqqqqqqqqqqqqqqqqqqqqqqqqqqqqqqqqqqklqqqqqqqqqqqqqqqqqqqqqqqqqqqqqqqqqqqqqqqk
x    Time:        2015-08-05T11:13:57.000Z   xxPRN:    Elev:   Azim:   SNR:   Used:  x
x    Latitude:     57.715973 N               xx  16     10     294     28      Y     x
x    Longitude:    11.974035 E               xx  23     13     325     24      Y     x
x    Altitude:    4.3 m                      xx   2     21     045     25      Y     x
x    Speed:       1.3 kph                    xx   9     06     358     25      Y     x
x    Heading:     4.0 deg (true)             xx  26     38     289     32      Y     x
x    Climb:       21.4 m/min                 xx  31     49     241     18      Y     x
x    Status:      3D FIX (87 secs)           xx                                      x
x    Longitude Err:   +/- 14 m               xx                                      x
x    Latitude Err:    +/- 35 m               xx                                      x
x    Altitude Err:    +/- 90 m               xx                                      x
x    Course Err:      n/a                    xx                                      x
x    Speed Err:       +/- 259 kph            xx                                      x
x    Time offset:     0.084                  xx                                      x
x    Grid Square:     JO57xr                 xx                                      x
mqqqqqqqqqqqqqqqqqqqqqqqqqqqqqqqqqqqqqqqqqqqqqqqjmqqqqqqqqqqqqqqqqqqqqqqqqqqqqqqqqqqqqj
```

The output from the cgps –s command

Here, you can see the GPS satellites that I, in particular, have in my view, and my latitude and longitude as well as other useful information that is available through the GPS system.

If you get a timeout error from the `cgps` command, you need to restart the GPS daemon using the following commands:

```
sudo killall gpsd
sudo gpsd /dev/ttyUSB0 -F /var/run/gpsd.sock
```

If you get this timeout even though you have rebooted the Pi, then you can put the following commands in **crontab**, but, there is even a better place to put these, which will be described later on:

```
    @reboot sudo killall gpsd
    @reboot sudo gpsd /dev/ttyUSB0 -F /var/run/gpsd.sock
```

It is possible to get the location information programmatically from Python as well. We will make use of this possibility later on. But for now, the following Python code in a file named `getgps.py` to test the Python `gps` library:

```
#! /usr/bin/python

from gps import *
import math

gpsd = gps(mode=WATCH_ENABLE) #starting the stream of info

count = 0
while count < 10:  # wait max 50 seconds
    gpsd.next()
    if gpsd.fix.latitude != 0 and not
math.isnan(gpsd.fix.latitude) :
        print gpsd.fix.latitude,gpsd.fix.longitude
        break
    count = count + 1
    time.sleep(5)
```

The only thing this tiny program does is to output the GPS location whenever there is one to report. We can call it using the `python getgps.py` command.

Collecting the car data

For the purpose of collecting the car data, we will use a standard **On-board diagnostics (OBD)** interface found on most cars and referred to as OBD-II or EOBD in Europe. These are equivalent standards used to connect to the OBD port of the car; you can also read diagnostics data and fault codes about the car from this port.

In 1996, the OBD-II specification was made mandatory for all cars manufactured and sold in the United States. The European Union followed suit in 2001 by making EOBD mandatory for all gasoline (petrol) vehicles sold in the European Union, followed by all diesel vehicles in 2003. In 2010, the HDOBD (heavy duty) specification was made mandatory for certain select commercial (non-passenger car) engines sold in the United States. Even China followed suit in 2008, and by then, some light vehicles in China were required by the Environmental Protection Administration Office to implement OBD.

On most cars, the OBD interface is found under the steering wheel. On a Toyota Aygo from 2008, it is found on the right-hand side under the steering wheel. Some car manufacturers do not have standard port connections. So, you might have to buy an extra OBD converter cable. The port in the car looks like this:

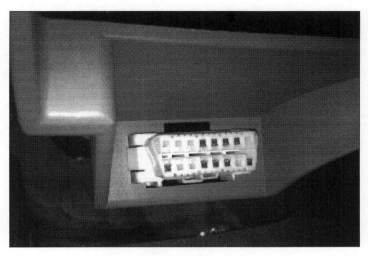

The OBD connection in the car

We will connect an **ELM327**-Bluetooth sender to this OBD connection and the Bluetooth dongle from the previous chapter to the Pi and make the two communicate. The ELM327 is a programmed microcontroller produced by **ELM Electronics** to translate the on-board diagnostics (OBD) interface. The ELM327 command protocol is one of the most popular PC-to-OBD interface standards implemented. You can buy one of these pieces of hardware in any price range with different properties on Amazon. The one that I have is by **Goliton**:

The ELM 327-OBD Bluetooth sender

The easiest way to get data from a car is to use an app on Android that can translate the data for you. Search for OBD on the Play Store, and you will find lots of great apps that can connect to ELM327 and show you all the details of your car data. However, we want to have a lot more fun than this.

Getting the car data to the Pi

To collect car data from the Pi using Python via Bluetooth, we need to install some tools. Run the following update command to download Bluetooth-related packages. Note that I am assuming that you have a **new Raspbian installation**. Same packages have been installed in previous chapters as well:

```
sudo apt-get install bluetooth bluez-utils blueman python-serial
python-wxgtk2.8 python-wxtools wx2.8-i18n libwxgtk2.8-dev git-core --
fix-missing
```

You are most probably sitting in your car and working right now. If you are struggling to figure out how to connect to the Internet, you can always use your Android device as a hotspot and connect to the Internet using the Wi-Fi dongle that we need for this chapter later on anyway.

Connecting the Pi to a Wi-Fi network was covered previously, but lets remind ourselves about how it works.

Add the following lines to the /etc/wpa_supplicant/wpa_supplicant.conf file. You need to have configured the hotspot to apply the WPA PSK security instead of PSK2:

```
network={
        ssid="YOUR_NETWORKID_FOR_HOTSPOT"
        psk="YOUR_PASSWORD_FOR_HOTSPOT"
}
```

Now, reboot the Pi, and after a few minutes, you will see that it is automatically connected to the hotspot on the Android device in the hotspot settings window.

Once again, we can use the lsusb command to list the connected USB devices. The output on my system is shown as follows:

```
Bus 001 Device 002: ID 0424:9514 Standard Microsystems Corp.
Bus 001 Device 001: ID 1d6b:0002 Linux Foundation 2.0 root hub
Bus 001 Device 003: ID 0424:ec00 Standard Microsystems Corp.
```

```
Bus 001 Device 004: ID 148f:5370 Ralink Technology, Corp. RT5370
Wireless Adapter

Bus 001 Device 005: ID 067b:2303 Prolific Technology, Inc. PL2303
Serial Port

Bus 001 Device 006: ID 0a5c:21e8 Broadcom Corp.
```

The `005` device is the Bluetooth dongle that I am reusing from the previous section. Issue the `hcitool scan` command to see if you can reach the OBD Bluetooth device connected to the car:

```
Scanning ...
        00:1D:A5:15:A0:DC           OBDII
```

You can see the MAC address of the OBD device as well; write it down as it will be used later.

> If you get into problems, such as scanning or reaching the OBD, you can use the following commands to see the status of the connected Bluetooth dongle and the `bluetooth` service on the Pi:
>
> `hciconfig hci0`
> `/etc/init.d/bluetooth status`
>
> Let's take a look at the following command:
> `/etc/init.d/bluetooth restart`
>
> The preceding command is used to restart the `bluetooth` service.

Now, we need to give the `pi` user access to the Bluetooth device. Edit the `/etc/group` file, find the row containing the `bluetooth` text, and add `pi` to the end of this row. It needs to look something similar to `bluetooth:x:113:pi`.

We can now connect the Pi's Bluetooth dongle to the OBD Bluetooth device using the `rfcomm` command. This command should be the first thing you execute before connecting to OBD. You can hang up before continuing using the *Ctrl+C* key combination:

```
sudo rfcomm connect hci0 00:1D:A5:15:A0:DC
```

Here, you should use the MAC address of your own ODB Bluetooth, which we found out previously using the `hcitool scan` command.

Now, issue the following Bluetooth pairing command to pair the Pi with OBD and use the MAC address of OBD:

```
sudo bluez-simple-agent hci0 00:1D:A5:15:A0:DC
```

The PIN is usually either 0000 or 1234:

```
RequestPinCode (/org/bluez/2336/hci0/dev_00_1D_A5_15_A0_DC)

Enter PIN Code: 1234

Release

New device (/org/bluez/2336/hci0/dev_00_1D_A5_15_A0_DC)
```

We should even add the dbus connection support before we continue to the next command:

```
sudo update-rc.d -f dbus defaults

sudo reboot
```

Make the OBD device trusted by the Pi in order to skip manual pairing the next time using the following command:

```
sudo bluez-test-device trusted 00:1D:A5:15:A0:DC yes
```

 The following command will let you test the connection if you have any problems. Replace the MAC address with your OBD adapter's MAC address:

```
sudo l2ping 00:1D:A5:15:A0:DC
```

We will use a tool, called pyOBD-pi, to access the data that the OBD dongle makes available. Download and start the logger using the git command. This is a more developer-friendly version of a well-known library located at https://github.com/peterh/pyobd:

```
git clone https://github.com/Pbartek/pyobd-pi

cd pyobd-pi

sudo python ./obd_recorder.py
```

 Do not forget to turn your ignition on. Also, don't forget to connect via Bluetooth using the upcoming command. It is a good idea to put this in crontab, otherwise, you'll need to use it every time you reboot the Pi:

```
sudo rfcomm connect hci0 00:1D:A5:15:A0:DC &
```

The command will save the data traffic to the `log` directory. If you get errors regarding `0100 response:CAN ERROR`, then you have problems with protocol selections, and you simply need to edit the `obd_io.py` file and find the following line:

```
self.send_command("0100")
```

Then, add the following lines of code just before it:

```
self.send_command("ATSP0")  # select auto protocol
wx.PostEvent(self._notify_window, DebugEvent([2,"ATSP0 response:"
+ self.get_result()]))
```

In this way, we have forced the communication protocol to be chosen automatically.

> You may want to run the `init` server script on reboot. You cannot put it in cronbtab as the Bluetooth or GPS might not be ready when it is run. Put the commands at the end of `/etc/rc.local` file before the exit line, instead:
>
> **sudo killall gpsd**
> **sudo gpsd /dev/ttyUSB0 -F /var/run/gpsd.sock**
> **sudo rfcomm connect hci0 00:1D:A5:15:A0:DC &**

Using your Android device as an access point

We will send the data we have gathered so far to a location on a cloud, but we need to connect the Pi to the Internet before we do this. Making an Android device an Internet access point or a hotspot is trivial and can be done from the settings of a device. We can then connect the Pi to this network that Android provides. However, there is a major problem with this setup. First of all, we want to be able to leave the Pi and the phone in the car all the time. As soon as the car starts, we want the data to be sent automatically, and we do not want to carry around the Pi and a phone. However, if we leave the phone in the car and it is connected to the 12V power output, the device will soon run out of battery and shut down. Then, we'll need to power it on manually and make changes in the hotspot settings again. We want all these steps to be undertaken automatically. For this reason, we need a way to get the device powered on as soon as it is connected to a power source, or the power source it is connected to, such as a 12V power output in the car, wakes up when we start the car. The techniques I will now present require that you have super user privileges to your Android device, which means that we need to root the device.

An alternative to rooting

An alternative to rooting a device is using a USB Wi-Fi 3G modem to get Internet access in the car. Note that most of the 3G USB modems in the market do not provide you with a Wi-Fi network. They only give network access to the computer into which they are plugged. The one we need acts similar to a Wi-Fi hotspot when connected to a USB power source. You can find these at online retailers, such as Amazon or AliExpress. The one I personally use is shown in the following image:

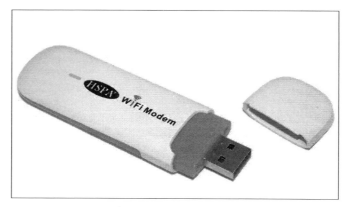

The USB Wi-Fi 3G modem

If you choose to use one of these, you may jump over the rest of this section and go directly to the next.

Rooting Samsung Galaxy S2

There are different ways of rooting different devices. I will use one of the most common second hand Android devices in the market, namely, Samsung Galaxy S2. If you have another phone, there are plenty of resources available on the Internet on how to root each device. The most popular one is located at http://www.androidcentral.com/root, the **Android Central** website.

Note that rooting a device will make the guarantee invalid. This may cause damage to your phone and is not a secure process. Do it on your own risk. But the steps provided here worked for me. You should backup any files you would like to keep before you continue with the rest of this chapter.

Samsung devices can be put into recovery mode by pressing the *volume down, power, home* buttons at the same time. By pressing these buttons, you will get Samsung's standard recovery screen with a warning sign on it. We should replace this recovery program with another one, as the standard recovery is only to be done through a computer connected via a USB and downloads a complete OS image. However, what we really need to do is only replace a kernel with one that gives us super user rights. We also want to make sure that we do this from an SD card attached to an Android device. That is why we need to replace Samsung's default recovery program. We can do this again using the recovery operation provided by Samsung.

When you put the device in this recovery mode, attach it to a computer through a USB. Next, we can download a software, named **Odin**, to upload a new recovery tool to the phone. It can be downloaded from quite a lot of places on the Internet along with different versions. The one we will use is called `ODIN3_v1.85.zip`, and it is located at `https://www.androidfilehost.com/?fid=9390169635556426736`. Another file we need is a kernel to replace the existing one that will help us with new ways of recovery operations. This file is named **Jeboo Kernel**, and can be found at `http://downloadandroidrom.com/file/GalaxyS2/kernels/JB/jeboo_kernel_i9100_v1-2a.tar`.

As instructed on the recovery screen on the phone, you should press the *volume up* button to put the device in the download mode. Then, start Odin, and select the newly downloaded Jeboo Kernel as **PDA**. You should see a COM box marked in yellow if the phone is correctly connected, and is in the kernel download mode:

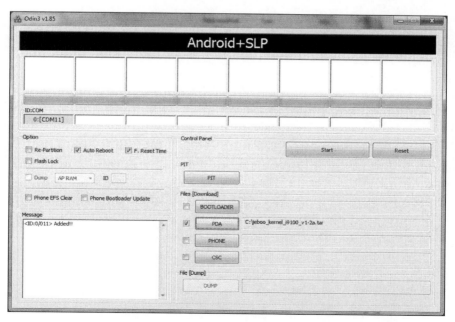

Odin shows Jeboo as PDA and a connected device on COM11. Click on **Start** to upload upload the new Jeboo kernel you have selected.

It should not take too much time before you get a **PASS** notification:

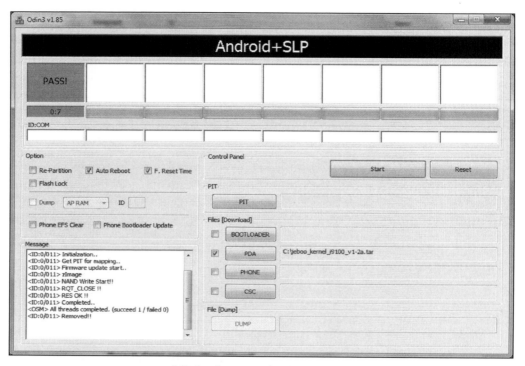

Odin has been completed successfully

Now, your phone should reboot, and you should see a warning triangle on the restart screen, indicating that you have a new kernel with the "recovery from SD card" feature.

The next step is to save the **CWM Super User** file from `http://downloadandroidrom.com/file/tools/SuperSU/CWM-SuperSU-v0.99.zip` to the SD card and attach it to the device. Now, power off your device and put it into recovery mode again this time using a slightly different key combination, that is, *volume up, power, home*. Note that we press *volume up* instead of *volume down* as we did before. You will see a different recovery screen called **CWM-based Recovery**. You can scroll up and down using the *volume up* and *volume down* keys. Select the **Install Zip** item using the *home* button, and then the **Choose from SD card** option. You should browse to the CWM Super User ZIP file that you have downloaded on to the SD card. Finally, choose **Yes**.

Reboot the device, and you will see a new app called **Super User**, which indicates that you have successfully rooted your device. You can even verify that you have super user access to your device by downloading one of the Super User checker apps on Google Play. You will see a message box asking you a question from the Super User app, that we had installed from the previous step, if you want to grant super user privileges to any other app asking to get those.

Enabling tethering on being connected to a power source

As our phone hypothetically stays in the car all the time, and only gets powered up when the car is being used, we need to find a way to enable Wi-Fi tethering or a hotspot, as it is as well called, whenever the phone is connected to a power source. There are two cases that we might encounter, though:

- The battery has run out and the phone is turned off at night. Here, we need to find a way to turn on the phone whenever it gets powered up again. This happens when we start the car. When the phone is successfully turned on, we need to find a way to enable a hotspot.

- The phone still has enough battery to keep it turned on, but as it hasn't been used, the hotspot is disabled. Note that the only device using the phone's hotspot is the Pi and it is turned off if the car isn't being used. When we start the car again, the phone gets powered up from the USB contact. In this case, we need to enable the hotspot again.

Automatic restart on power connect

When we connect a turned off Samsung device to a power source, we will see a gray battery image with a turning arrow inside it. Then, when it begins charging the battery, we will see another colored battery image showing the current charge level. This second image is generated by a program that is triggered whenever a turned off device begins charging the battery. It is a binary file located in /system/bin/ playlpm on the phone. We will change this file to a script of our own to reboot the device. In order to be able to edit this file, we need super user privileges. This is why we have rooted the phone. As an Android system is actually a Linux OS under the hood, we can run any Linux command on it. We can do this using an app that we can download from the Play Store, called **Terminal Emulator**:

The Terminal Emulator app screen

Now, issue the upcoming commands to change the contents of the playlpm file and make it an executable file. We need to also remount the /system directory in order to enable it for write operations:

```
mount -o rw,remount /system
mv playlpm playlpmbackup
echo "#!/system/bin/sh" > playlpm
echo "sleep 60" >> playlpm
```

```
echo "/system/bin/reboot" >> playlpm
chmod 0755 /system/bin/playlpm
chown root.shell /system/bin/playlpm
mount -o ro,remount /system
```

Turn off the device and connect it to a power source. You will see that it turns on automatically after one minute. We have introduced the one minute delay because if the battery is totally discharged, it will not have enough capacity to restart the device. We want to wait at least one minute in these kinds of situations for the battery to get charged enough to restart the device. If it is not charged sufficiently, you might need to charge your phone before it can automatically restart. You can charge the phone without getting it restarted by putting it in to the recovery mode and then begin charging it.

Auto tethering

Now we are able to restart the device on connecting it to a power source. We need to also enable tethering on the device when it wakes up or is connected to a power source. There are apps on the market that already do this, but the best ones are paid. This is one of the reasons that we will implement our own app for this purpose. The other reason is that it is fun.

We can create a new application in the Android Studio as we did before. We will not need any Activity for this application.

Create a new java file, called StartTetheringAtBootReceiver, for BroadcastReceiver and add the following code in it:

```
public class StartTetheringAtBootReceiver extends
BroadcastReceiver {
    public static void setWifiTetheringEnabled(boolean enable,
Context context) {
        WifiManager wifiManager = (WifiManager)
context.getSystemService(Context.WIFI_SERVICE);

        Method[] methods =
          wifiManager.getClass().getDeclaredMethods();
        for (Method method : methods) {
          if (method.getName().equals("setWifiApEnabled")) {
              try {
                    method.invoke(wifiManager, null, enable);
              } catch (Exception ex) {
                  ex.printStackTrace();
              }
              break;
```

```
        }
      }
    }
     @Override
    public void onReceive(Context context, Intent intent) {
        if (Intent.ACTION_BOOT_COMPLETED.equals(intent.getAction())
|| Intent.ACTION_POWER_CONNECTED.equals(intent.getAction())) {
          setWifiTetheringEnabled(true, context);
        }
      }
    }
```

This piece of code receives broadcast events whenever the phone is booted or connected to a power source, and enables tethering on the device with the default settings. If we'd like to change the name of the network or the password, we'll need to modify the settings on the device.

Add the manifest definition for the new broadcast receiver to AndroidManifest.xml inside the application tag:

```
<receiver
android:name=".StartTetheringAtBootReceiver"
   android:label="StartTetheringAtBootReceiver">
   <intent-filter>
      <action android:name="android.intent.action.BOOT_COMPLETED"
/>
      <action
android:name="android.intent.action.ACTION_POWER_CONNECTED" />
   </intent-filter>
</receiver>
```

Add the following permission declarations inside the manifest tag:

```
<uses-permission
android:name="android.permission.CHANGE_WIFI_STATE"/>
<uses-permission
android:name="android.permission.RECEIVE_BOOT_COMPLETED" />
```

Now, install this app to your phone and see if the tethering is enabled whenever you reboot the device or connect a power cable to it.

We can optionally add a shortcut button for tethering in MainActivity. In the activity_main.xml file, add the following button definition:

```
<Button android:text="@string/enable"
        android:layout_width="wrap_content"
        android:layout_height="wrap_content"
        android:onClick="click"/>
```

Next, in the `MainAcitivty.java` file, define the handler for the button:

```
public void click(View v) {
    StartTetheringAtBootReceiver
        .setWifiTetheringEnabled(true, this);
}
```

Next, we need to connect the Pi to the hotspot that we have created so far. Connecting the Pi to a Wi-Fi network was covered earlier, but let's remind ourselves about this concept again. Add the upcoming lines of code to the /etc/ wpa_supplicant/wpa_supplicant.conf file. We can configure the hotspot to apply WPA PSK security instead of PSK2:

```
network={
        ssid="YOUR_NETWORKID_FOR_HOTSPOT"
        psk="YOUR_PASSWORD_FOR_HOTSPOT"
}
```

Now, we'll reboot the Pi, and after a few minutes, we'll see that it is automatically connected to a hotspot on the Android device in the hotspot settings window:

The list of connected devices is shown in hotspot settings in Android

You must be wondering why we have covered this content at this point. This is because in order to implement the next section, you'll most probably need to sit in your car and communicate with the Pi inside your car, where you most probably do not have more network access than the hotspot Android provides you with. Now, if you connect to the same hotspot on Android from your computer, you will be able to SSH to the Pi with a tool called **PuTTY** that you can install on Windows machines or using built in SSH terminal tool on a Mac.

Sending data to the cloud

We will use a Google Docs spreadsheet to save data and a special Python library developed for this purpose. We begin doing this by creating an API key to access Google services.

Browse to `https://console.developers.google.com/project` and create an account for this purpose. When it's ready, you will be directed to the Google Developer Console:

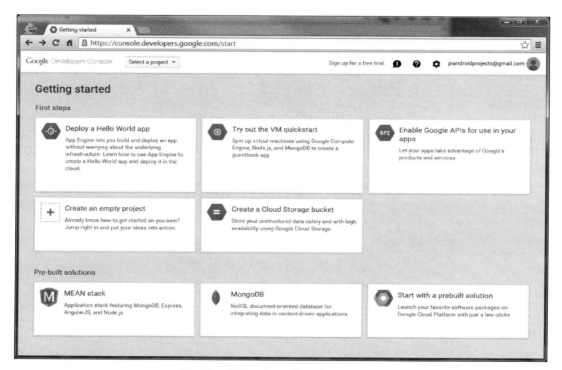

The Google Developer Console start page

Here, we'll need to create a new project in the **Select a project** drop-down menu. Give it a suitable name, accept the agreement, and click on **Create**. Select the newly created project, **APIs & auth**, and then select **APIs** from the menu on the left-hand side. Then, find and select **Drive API**, and press the **Enable API** button. When it is enabled, go to **Credentials** on the left-hand side menu under **APIs & auth**:

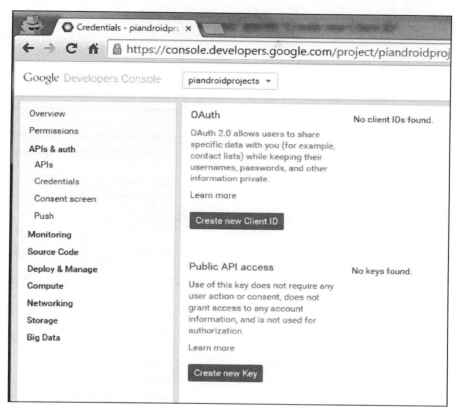

The menu to enable OAuth in the Google Developer Console

Here, under **OAuth**, click on the **Create new Client ID** button. In the message box that appears, select the **Service account**, and click on the **Create Client ID** button. We'll see a box telling us that we have successfully created **New public/private key pair** for the project. We'll even see that the site has sent us a **JSON** file with credentials in it. For the dummy account I created, the contents looks similar to this:

```
{
    "private_key_id": "ed5a741ff85f235167015d99a1adc3033f0e6f9f",
    "private_key": "-----BEGIN PRIVATE KEY-----\
nMIIEvgIBADANBgkqhkiG9w0BAQEFAASCBKgwggSkAgEAAoIBAQDM9YJ2otxwdhcL
\nQJ8ipZOuILkq9dzWDJJgtjSgFUXTJvjgzTDNa2WXGy9p9i4Wuzrj5OJli/M5dMWr
\n+CVZCpsfV7Xt7iqkeCEo0dN225HDiAXXMvWKhDsiofau0xLCTFLDnLZFWqAd55ec
\naENYQKp6ZEc6dGaA7Kp7O1+7LtEB2a4yqgZIelL6fTSSLQqyV477OS2Dkq+nz5Sz
\nRyTexcDWioDNp2vdGadqDfRKsI7ELwgWscaV6jrbHz2uDuC844UnTL4WKMugp1n1
\nObTuGDl1gldEIWlk2XSLFkGfY30lYV7XwrUQGgc85AGRwdH7qYrQM3jO4D+6thAH
\nETq4qjRRAgMBAAECggEAJjXXHrr6EdVSMnzXriPkRmA/ZSz1AMrTN0iAwx90Jwtq
\n9q4KXSGajPM6gaytpvs83WO8eWX/8EQ+3fKjM9hwVwWJG1R9irACrpN/svb4U9W2
\nEQqlEC/avngnfyxGoQaNn35F1OQyWaDlePlPJNLZdXvgc5tjyMFWfybwj/sIaCmR
\nnj5ntV2aY/gCEbe6km7L/LkC3C7CesIWstUGMHCjh2aPeQT+Hpodf23AnLZuSo34j
\nB+lSI/RjnDsd0HfazOgaOXa/yK4SliTaMWUBiMSXQcwZZsVp/RL0Ve6W2PSfi092
\n+hATaaRnA8zB8fx7PnAltPhFwVr9+jjbYbq+wypoyQKBgQDoLJytaR4wof46MUiL
\nMWrXDopi5dG2ofUSXR+JEIThe7yyYepzzdWFL+rXNEzD5X9UcfCodwZ0PKLN3u0t
\nZJ5Iq111bxwwZix5uVStRi6stgGaewF6nkDqN8y5TJJgnZB9wSBuG3RvCU4zwXKZ
\nngj2+azWme7PSyOHKNODbBd9DkwKBgQDh/e7nct49/Z0Om/+kNJ+NXUjka+S1yF7n
\nhL+HZ2WU1gL8iQjXPxnCX1lThw7C4rForH/esOs+f1XMje8NYi7ggslqxoXwFRH6
\nny/tuCRaY+e62xmJAxj2o8InsvQQkSM+dtuZiaNq3gCatHKbx2C6SVQal/y3yuR0c
\nn00adgr6fCwKBgQDSlAvzGIFiWLsNqr+CR+sAbVbExm9EN3bhFgdROONc4+7M2BRe
\nnvlUoPMLCN9RcZR3syH8fPP1klc6P7N6vqjAJ9yuIJKOrnjA+owKTOjGBQn8HzwMT
\nnZM+536xWcIXfDWoNNQol887SGt2MAavgYYmA2RpLCq2Zw8tOrFE5NgU+8wKBgQCe
\nAiwNy3S0JySu2EevidOcxYJ3ozBwIT6p5Vj81UBjBhdkdnOl+8qI6p3MFvwtKs8b
\n/rARBeYU9ncI5Jwl4WYhN5CYhWGUcUb28bRERTp1jxpm1OJRo8ns2vG0gpvourfe
\n78i5OdLixklEdGoNYjd9vNE/MuHveZpvUxFmg8m/7QKBgCGVTkOXWLpRxuYT+M+M
\n28LBgftHxu0YZdXx8mU9x6LQYG2aFxho7bkEYiEaNYJn51kdNZqzrIHebxT/dh/z
\nddd5nR93E6WsPuqstZF4ZhJ+l2m77wmG9u5gfRifrNpc3TK0IswydFPIMNVxMz+d
\nl3cdqtiW6rvWSQoHC0brpcYL\n-----END PRIVATE KEY-----\n",
    "client_email": "14902682557-
05eecriag0m9jbo50ohnt59sest5694d@developer.gserviceaccount.com",
    "client_id": "14902682557-
05eecriag0m9jbo50ohnt59sest5694d.apps.googleusercontent.com",
    "type": "service_account"
}
```

We can choose to generate a new key from the Developer Console site using the **Generate new JSON key** button for our project.

At this stage, we need to generate a **P12** key using the **Generate new P12 key** button. This file will be used later on. We will also be provided with a secret key when we download the file which we need to note down. The following screenshot illustrates the Google Developer Console after successful creation of the API key:

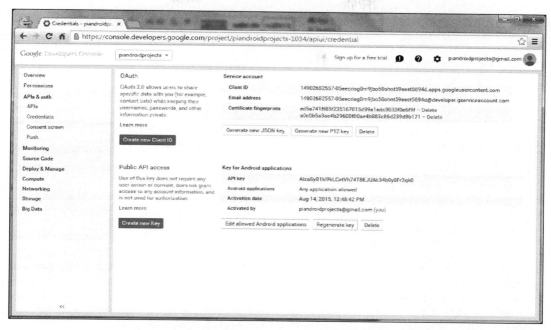

Google Developer Console after successful API key creations

Before we can install the Google Python library, we need to install a tool, called `pip`, which will help us install an OAuth client we will use to connect to Google services. Use the following commands to do this:

```
curl -O
https://raw.githubusercontent.com/pypa/pip/master/contrib/get-pip.py
sudo python get-pip.py
```

Then, use this new `pip` tool to install the OAuth clients:

```
sudo apt-get update
sudo apt-get install build-essential libssl-dev libffi-dev python-dev
sudo pip install --upgrade oauth2client
sudo pip install PyOpenSSL
```

The next step is to download and install the client library to access Google Sheets on the Pi using the following commands:

```
git clone https://github.com/burnash/gspread.git
cd gspread
sudo python setup.py install
```

Before we begin coding, we need to add a new spreadsheet on the `https://docs.google.com` website. Select **Sheets** in the menu, create a new sheet using the plus (**+**) sign, and change the name from `Untitled spreadsheet` to `CAR_OBD_SHEET`. It should be saved automatically. We need to share this spreadsheet with the Google Developer Console client created for us when we generated the OAuth key pair. We'll find a `client_email` field in the JSON file we've downloaded. We will share the new spreadsheet with this client. Now, open the `CAR_OBD_SHEET` spreadsheet in Google Docs and click on the **Share** button:

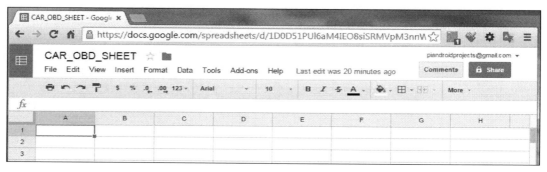

Open the spreadsheet in Google Docs

In the pop-up window, paste `client_email` from the JSON file, then click on the **Send** button on the pop-up window. This will share the spreadsheet with the client generated when we created the OAuth key pair in the previous step:

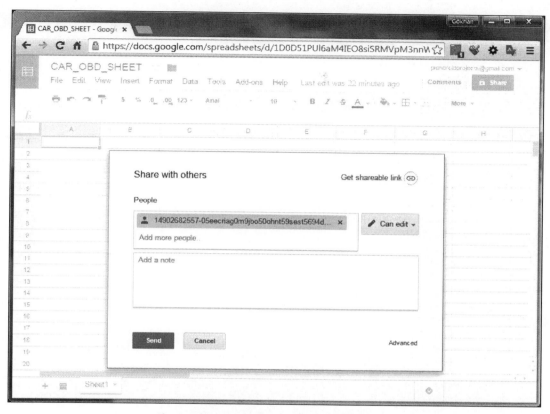

Sharing the spreadsheet with the generated client

Now, we will test to see if everything works fine. Create a file on the Pi, name it `send_to_sheet.py`, and put the following content in it. Do not forget to create the OAuth JSON file and put the contents of the one we have downloaded from the Google Developer Console and name it as `piandroidprojects.json`:

```
import json
import gspread
from datetime import datetime
from oauth2client.client import SignedJwtAssertionCredentials

json_key = json.load(open('piandroidprojects.json'))
scope = ['https://spreadsheets.google.com/feeds']

credentials =
SignedJwtAssertionCredentials(json_key['client_email'],
json_key['private_key'], scope)

gc = gspread.authorize(credentials)
t = datetime.now()
sh = gc.open("CAR_OBD_SHEET").add_worksheet(str(t.year) + "_" +
str(t.month) + "_" + str(t.day) + "_" + str(t.hour) + "_" +
str(t.minute) + "_" + str(t.second), 100, 20)

sh.update_cell(1, 1, 0.23)
```

Now, run the file using the `python send_to_sheet.py` command, and we will see the update on the Google Docs sheet. The code will create a new worksheet named as the current timestamp and save a single value in this sheet. Note that Google allows 200 worksheets per sheet, and by default, 100 rows per worksheet; in our code, we create a new worksheet each time we run it. We need to clean the sheet from time to time in order to not to go beyond the limit.

Putting it all together

In the next two sections, we will put together what we have done so far. First, we'll begin by sending data to the Google Docs sheet. Then, we will build an Android app to show the data on a map.

Sending measurements

We will use a Python script to access GPS data on the Pi that we'll need to run on system reboot. For this purpose, add the following code at the end of the /etc/rc.local file:

```
sudo killall gpsd
sudo gpsd /dev/ttyUSB0 -F /var/run/gpsd.sock
sudo rfcomm connect hci0 00:1D:A5:15:A0:DC &
sleep 1m
current_time=$(date "+%Y.%m.%d-%H.%M.%S")
file_name=/home/pi/log_sender.txt
new_filename=$file_name.$current_time
sudo /home/pi/pyobd-pi/sender.py > $new_filename 2>&1 &
```

Here, we can restart the GPS services, connect to the OBD Bluetooth dongle, create a log file, and start the sender.py script that we will implement next:

```python
#!/usr/bin/env python

import obd_io
from datetime import datetime
import time
import threading
import commands
import time
from gps import *
import math
import json
import gspread
from oauth2client.client import SignedJwtAssertionCredentials

gpsd = None

class GpsPoller(threading.Thread):
    def __init__(self):
        threading.Thread.__init__(self)
        global gpsd
        gpsd = gps(mode=WATCH_ENABLE)

    def run(self):
        global gpsd
        while True:
```

```
            gpsd.next()


class OBD_Sender():
    def __init__(self):
        self.port = None
        self.sensorlist = [3,4,5,12,13,31,32]

    def connect(self):
        self.port = obd_io.OBDPort("/dev/rfcomm0", None, 2, 2)
        if(self.port):
            print "Connected to "+str(self.port)

    def is_connected(self):
        return self.port

    def get_data(self):
        if(self.port is None):
            return None
        current = 1
        while 1:
            cell_list = []

            localtime = datetime.now()
            cell = sh.cell(current, 1)
            cell.value = localtime
            cell_list.append(cell)

            try:
                gpsd.next()
            except:
                print "gpsd.next() error"

            cell = sh.cell(current, 2)
            cell.value = gpsd.fix.latitude
            cell_list.append(cell)

            cell = sh.cell(current, 3)
            cell.value = gpsd.fix.longitude
            cell_list.append(cell)

            column = 4
            for index in self.sensorlist:
```

```
            (name, value, unit) = self.port.sensor(index)
            cell = sh.cell(current, column)
            cell.value = value
            cell_list.append(cell)
            column = column + 1

        try:
            sh.update_cells(cell_list)
            print "sent data"
        except:
            print "update_cells error"

        current = current + 1
        time.sleep(10)

json_key = json.load(open('/home/pi/pyobd-
pi/piandroidprojects.json'))
scope = ['https://spreadsheets.google.com/feeds']

credentials =
SignedJwtAssertionCredentials(json_key['client_email'],
json_key['private_key'], scope)

while True:
    try:
        gc = gspread.authorize(credentials)
        break
    except:
        print "Error in GoogleDocs authorize"

t = datetime.now()
sh = gc.open("CAR_OBD_SHEET").add_worksheet(str(t.year)+"_"+str(t.
month
)+"_"+str(t.day)+"_"+str(t.hour)+"_"+str(t.minute)+"_"+str(t.secon
d), 100, 20)

gpsp = GpsPoller()
gpsp.start()

o = OBD_Sender()
o.connect()
time.sleep(5)
o.connect()
time.sleep(5)
o.get_data()
```

The code begins running at the end where we define `json_key` by loading the JSON key file. Then, we'll try to authorize using the `gspread.authorize(credentials)` method. The next step is to create a new worksheet with the date timestamp as the title, and then start to consume the GPS data in another thread defined by the `GpsPoller` class. Next, we'll initiate the `OBD_Sender` class and connect to the ODB Bluetooth device twice. The connect operation may fail when it's executed for the first time, but it almost always succeeds when it's run a second time. Then, we need to run the `get_data` method of the `OBD_Sender` class to begin the loop.

The `GpsPoller` class consumes all the values of the GPS device connected to the serial USB port. This is required in order to get the most recent values whenever we access the `gpsd.fix.latitude` and `gpsd.fix.longitude` variables.

The `get_data` method of the `OBD_Sender` class sends the local time, latitude, and longitude values to the spreadsheet, and it also sends seven different readings defined in `self.sensorlist = [3,4,5,12,13,31,32]`. We can see these values from the SENSORS list in the `obd_sensors.py` file. For your information, these are the Fuel System Status, Calculated Load Value, Coolant Temp, Engine RPM, Vehicle Speed, Engine Start MIN, and Engine Run MIL values. We can change the indexes to read the values that we want. Take a look at additional values at `https://en.wikipedia.org/wiki/OBD-II_PIDs`. We go through these codes, read their current values, and send them to the different cells of a current row on our worksheet. After starting and driving your car around, you can see that the data is uploaded to the spreadsheet, as shown in the following screenshot:

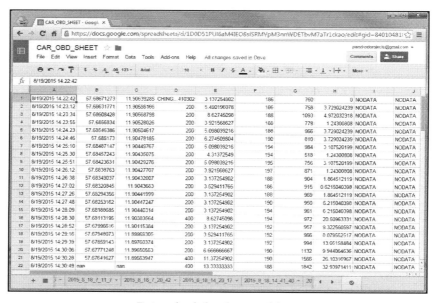

Data uploaded to the spreadsheet

Retrieving measurements

We will build our very own app to download the measurement values and show them on a map. Create a new blank project in the Android Studio, and choose to include a Google Maps Activity during the last step of create project wizard. I've used Android 4.3 as the base SDK for this project; I will name my main activity as MapsActivity.

To access Google Docs and download the content of the spreadsheet, we will use some of the Java libraries provided by Google. They are located at different places. Download the ZIP files from the following locations:

- A general purpose Java client for Google data services is located at https://github.com/google/gdata-java-client, and the file is named as gdata-src.java-*.zip, which is found under the **Source** link.

- Download the HTTP client from https://developers.google.com/api-client-library/java/google-http-java-client/download which is named as google-http-java-client-featured.zip. We will use this to authorize ourselves.

- Download the OAuth client contained in google-oauth-java-client-featured.zip, which is available at https://developers.google.com/api-client-library/java/google-oauth-java-client/download

Now, open these ZIP files, locate the following JAR libraries, and move them to the libs folder under your Android app directory:

- gdata-base-1.0.jar
- gdata-core-1.0.jar
- gdata-spreadsheet-3.0.jar
- google-api-client-1.20.0.jar
- google-http-client-1.20.0.jar
- google-http-client-jackson-1.20.0.jar
- google-oauth-client-1.20.0.jar
- guava-11.0.2.jar
- jackson-core-asl-1.9.11.jar

To include these libraries in your Android project, you need to add them to the `build.gradle` file for `Module:app`. To do this, add the following code under the `dependencies` tag.

```
compile files('libs/gdata-spreadsheet-3.0.jar')
compile files('libs/gdata-core-1.0.jar')
compile files('libs/guava-11.0.2.jar')
compile files('libs/gdata-base-1.0.jar')
compile files('libs/google-http-client-1.20.0.jar')
compile files('libs/google-http-client-jackson-1.20.0.jar')
compile files('libs/google-api-client-1.20.0.jar')
compile files('libs/google-oauth-client-1.20.0.jar')
compile files('libs/jackson-core-asl-1.9.11.jar')
```

When you edit the `build.gradle` file, you might get a message in Android, stating that **Gradle files has changed since last project sync. A project sync maybe necessary for the IDE to work properly**. Click on the **Sync Now** link located near this notification to update the project.

The next step is to move the `P12` key file, which we have downloaded from the Google Developer Console, and include it in our Android project. We need to copy this file in the `raw` directory located at `PROJECT_HOME\app\src\main\res\raw` and rename it as `piandroidprojects.p12`.

As we plan to show the content on a map, we will use Google's Map API for this purpose. To use it, we need an access API key. Go to the developer console again at `https://console.developers.google.com/project`, and select the project that we've created previously. In the menu located on the left-hand side, choose **APIs** under **APIS & auth**, then, **Google Maps Android API**, and finally, click on the **Enable API** button. Next, navigate to **Credentials**, and click on the **Create new key** button under the **Public API access** section. We need to choose **Android key** in the window that pops up. Copy the generated **API key** and replace it with the `YOUR_KEY_HERE` string in the `google_maps_api.xml` file. Now, we are ready with our Android project setup, and it is time to code now.

The first thing to do in the code is download a list of sheets from Google Docs. There is one sheet for each restart of the Pi. Add the following code inside the `onCreate` method of the `MapsActivity.java` file:

```
new RetrieveSpreadsheets().execute();
```

This piece of code will create an asynchronous task that is implemented as an Android `AsyncTask`, which downloads and presents the spreadsheets. Let's define the task class in the same file as well:

```java
class RetrieveSpreadsheets extends AsyncTask<Void, Void,
List<WorksheetEntry>> {
    @Override
    protected List<WorksheetEntry> doInBackground(Void params) {
        try {
            service =
                new SpreadsheetService("MySpreadsheetIntegration-v1");
            HttpTransport httpTransport = new NetHttpTransport();
            JacksonFactory jsonFactory = new JacksonFactory();
            String[] SCOPESArray =
                {"https://spreadsheets.google.com/feeds",
                 "https://spreadsheets.google.com/feeds/spreadsheets/p
                  rivate/full",
                 "https://docs.google.com/feeds"};
            final List SCOPES = Arrays.asList(SCOPESArray);
            KeyStore keystore = KeyStore.getInstance("PKCS12");
            keystore.load(
                getResources().openRawResource(R.raw.piandroidproject
            s), "notasecret".toCharArray());
            PrivateKey key = (PrivateKey)
        keystore.getKey("privatekey", "notasecret".toCharArray());

            GoogleCredential credential =
                new GoogleCredential.Builder()
                    .setTransport(httpTransport)
                    .setJsonFactory(jsonFactory)
                    .setServiceAccountPrivateKey(key)
                    .setServiceAccountId("14902682557-
        05eecriag0m9jbo50ohnt59sest5694d@developer.gserviceaccount.com")
                    .setServiceAccountScopes(SCOPES)
                    .build();

            service.setOAuth2Credentials(credential);
            URL SPREADSHEET_FEED_URL = new
        URL("https://spreadsheets.google.com/feeds/spreadsheets/
        private/full");
            SpreadsheetFeed feed =
                service.getFeed(SPREADSHEET_FEED_URL,
            SpreadsheetFeed.class);
```

```
            List<SpreadsheetEntry> spreadsheets = feed.getEntries();

            return spreadsheets.get(0).getWorksheets();

        } catch (MalformedURLException e) {
          e.printStackTrace();
        } catch (ServiceException e) {
          e.printStackTrace();
        } catch (IOException e) {
          e.printStackTrace();
        } catch (GeneralSecurityException e) {
          e.printStackTrace();
        }
        return null;
    }


    protected void onPostExecute(final List<WorksheetEntry>
worksheets) {
        if(worksheets == null || worksheets.size() == 0) {
            Toast.makeText(MapsActivity.this, "Nothing saved yet",
Toast.LENGTH_LONG).show();
        } else {
            final List<String> worksheetTitles =
                new ArrayList<String>();
            for(WorksheetEntry worksheet : worksheets) {
              worksheetTitles.add(
                  worksheet.getTitle().getPlainText());
            }

            AlertDialog.Builder alertDialogBuilder =
                new AlertDialog.Builder(MapsActivity.this);
            alertDialogBuilder.setTitle("Select a worksheet");
            alertDialogBuilder.setAdapter(
                new ArrayAdapter<String>(
                    MapsActivity.this,
                    android.R.layout.simple_list_item_1,
                    worksheetTitles.toArray(new String[0])),
                    new DialogInterface.OnClickListener() {
                      @Override
                      public void onClick(DialogInterface dialog, int
                    which) {
                          new RetrieveWorksheetContent()
                              .execute(worksheets.get(which));
                      }
                });
```

```
            alertDialogBuilder.create().show();
    }
        }
    }
```

Before we describe the preceding code, define an instance variable for the spreadsheet service, which is used in the task we have just defined:

```
SpreadsheetService service;
```

The Android `AsyncTask` requires us to override the `doInBackground` method, which is executed in a new thread whenever we call the `execute` method of the task that we performed in `onCreate`. In `doInBackground`, we will define `KeyStore`, and load the `P12` file that we've downloaded from the Google Developer Console and copied to the `raw` directory of our Android project. Note that `notasecret` was the secret that the Developer Console informed me about when I created and downloaded the `P12` file. Also, inside the `setServiceAccountId` method, you'll need to use your own account name. You can find it in the Developer Console under the **Service account** section in the **Email address** field as well as in the JSON key file **client_email** field. In the background method, after loading the key file and defining the credentials, we'll authorize ourselves to Google Spreadsheets service using OAuth. We'll simply get the first spreadsheet that I assume is `CAR_OBD_SHEET` and return the worksheets in it. We could go through all the spreadsheets and search for the title as well, but I will skip this part of the code and assume that you have only one spreadsheet in your account with the title as `CAR_OBD_SHEET`.

The second function we'll define is `onPostExecute`. This function is called inside the UI thread by the Android system whenever background processing is performed. It is important that this is run in the UI thread as we cannot touch UI elements if we run UI-related code in non-UI threads.

Note here that the return value of the `doInBackground` method is sent as a parameter to the `onPostExecute` method, which is a list of worksheets found in a sheet in the Google Docs service. We'll go through this list and collect the titles in another list. Then, we'll show this list in a pop-up dialog box, which a user can click on and select. Whenever the user selects one of the worksheets, Android calls the `onClick` method of `DialogInterface.OnClickListener`, which we have sent in as a parameter to the adapter of `AlertDialog`. This method calls the `execute` method of another `AsyncTask` that we'll call `RetrieveWorksheetContent`, which, as the name implies, retrieves the content of the selected worksheet. Here is the definition for this task:

```
class RetrieveWorksheetContent extends AsyncTask<WorksheetEntry,
Void, List<List<Object>>> {

    @Override
```

```
    protected List<List<Object>> doInBackground(WorksheetEntry
params) {
        WorksheetEntry worksheetEntry = params[0];
        URL listFeedUrl= worksheetEntry.getListFeedUrl();
        List<List<Object>> values = new ArrayList<List<Object>>();
        try {
            ListFeed feed =
                service.getFeed(listFeedUrl, ListFeed.class);
            for(ListEntry entry : feed.getEntries()) {
                List<Object> rowValues = new ArrayList<Object>();
                for (String tag :
            entry.getCustomElements().getTags()) {
                    Object value =
                        entry.getCustomElements().getValue(tag);
                    rowValues.add(value);
                }
                values.add(rowValues);
            }
        } catch (IOException e) {
            e.printStackTrace();
        } catch (ServiceException e) {
            e.printStackTrace();
        }
        return values;
    }


    @Override
    protected void onPostExecute(List<List<Object>> values) {
        setUpMap(values);
        super.onPostExecute(values);
    }
}
```

Here, the most important part is where we iterate through `feed.getEntries()`, which refers to all the rows in the spreadsheet and the part where we iterate through `entry.getCustomElements().getTags()`, refers to all the columns. Then, in `onPostExecute`, we'll call the `setUpMap` method with all the values that we have retrieved. Inside this method, we'll create markers on the map that is contained in **MapsActivity**. Comment out the automatically defined `setUpMap` method if you do not want a marker at location 0,0, which Android Studio has defined for you as an example:

```
private void setUpMap(List<List<Object>> values) {
    for(List<Object> value : values) {
        String title = values.get(0).toString();
        try {
```

```
        double latitude =
            Double.parseDouble(value.get(1).toString());
        double longitude =
            Double.parseDouble(value.get(2).toString());
        if (latitude != 0 && longitude != 0)
            mMap.addMarker(
                new MarkerOptions().position(
                    new LatLng(latitude, longitude)))
                .setTitle(title);
    } catch(NumberFormatException ex) {
    }
  }
}
```

When you start the app, you will see a list of spreadsheets to choose from:

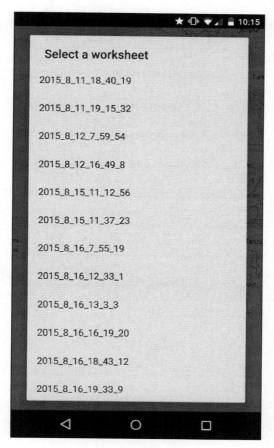

The list of spreadsheets

Next, after selecting one of these sheets, you can see the data on the map:

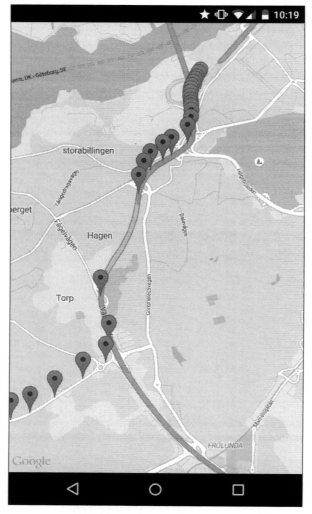

The data points on the map

Summary

In this chapter, we covered a lot of content, ranging from car diagnostics to Android device root process. We even covered a lot of Android code.

I hope that all of you have fun implementing these exciting projects, will try to enhance them and making them better than I did.

Index

A

Android Central
  URL 92
Android device
  automatic restart, on power connect 96, 97
  auto tethering 97-100
  data, sending to cloud 100-106
  rooting, alternative 92
  Samsung Galaxy S2, rooting 92-94
  tethering, enabling 95
  using, as access point 91
Android phone
  commands, sending to Pi 72
  reboot command, sending to Pi 70-72
Android Studio
  URL 63

B

BLE Scanner app 57, 63
BluePixel Technologies LLP 57
Bluetooth Low Energy (BLE) 53
  Android app, connecting from 63-69
  commands, combining 79, 80
  LED command, lighting 73-76
  more commands, sending from Android
      phone to Pi 72
  necessary components, installing 53-58
  reboot command, sending from Android
      phone to Pi 70-72
  sensor service, adding 59-62
  sound command, playing 77, 78
  versions, URL 54

C

camera
  hardware configurations 34
  software configurations 34
car data
  collecting 86-88
  collecting, from Pi 88-91
car location
  finding out 83-86
ConnectBot 14, 17
cron 27
crontab 27
CWM Super User file 95

D

data
  sending, to cloud 100-106
database
  and web server, implementation 22
  installing 25-27

E

ELM327-Bluetooth 87

F

files
  exchanging, between Pi and
      Android 17-22

G

Generic Attribute Profile (Gatt) 56

Thank you for buying
Raspberry Pi Android Projects

About Packt Publishing

Packt, pronounced 'packed', published its first book, *Mastering phpMyAdmin for Effective MySQL Management*, in April 2004, and subsequently continued to specialize in publishing highly focused books on specific technologies and solutions.

Our books and publications share the experiences of your fellow IT professionals in adapting and customizing today's systems, applications, and frameworks. Our solution-based books give you the knowledge and power to customize the software and technologies you're using to get the job done. Packt books are more specific and less general than the IT books you have seen in the past. Our unique business model allows us to bring you more focused information, giving you more of what you need to know, and less of what you don't.

Packt is a modern yet unique publishing company that focuses on producing quality, cutting-edge books for communities of developers, administrators, and newbies alike. For more information, please visit our website at www.packtpub.com.

About Packt Open Source

In 2010, Packt launched two new brands, Packt Open Source and Packt Enterprise, in order to continue its focus on specialization. This book is part of the Packt Open Source brand, home to books published on software built around open source licenses, and offering information to anybody from advanced developers to budding web designers. The Open Source brand also runs Packt's Open Source Royalty Scheme, by which Packt gives a royalty to each open source project about whose software a book is sold.

Writing for Packt

We welcome all inquiries from people who are interested in authoring. Book proposals should be sent to author@packtpub.com. If your book idea is still at an early stage and you would like to discuss it first before writing a formal book proposal, then please contact us; one of our commissioning editors will get in touch with you.

We're not just looking for published authors; if you have strong technical skills but no writing experience, our experienced editors can help you develop a writing career, or simply get some additional reward for your expertise.

Learning Raspberry Pi

ISBN: 978-1-78398-282-0   Paperback: 258 pages

Unlock your creative programming potential by creating web technologies, image processing, electronics- and robotics-based projects using the Raspberry Pi

1. Learn how to create games, web, and desktop applications using the best features of the Raspberry Pi.

2. Discover the powerful development tools that allow you to cross-compile your software and build your own Linux distribution for maximum performance.

3. Step-by-step tutorials show you how to quickly develop real-world applications using the Raspberry Pi.

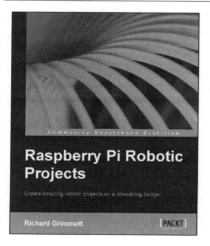

Raspberry Pi Robotic Projects

ISBN: 978-1-84969-432-2   Paperback: 278 pages

Create amazing robotic projects on a shoestring budget

1. Make your projects talk and understand speech with Raspberry Pi.

2. Use standard webcam to make your projects see and enhance vision capabilities.

3. Full of simple, easy-to-understand instructions to bring your Raspberry Pi online for developing robotics projects.

Please check **www.PacktPub.com** for information on our titles

Raspberry Pi for Secret Agents

ISBN: 978-1-84969-578-7   Paperback: 152 pages

Turn your Raspberry Pi into your very own secret agent toolbox with this set of exciting projects!

1. Detect an intruder on camera and set off an alarm.

2. Listen in or record conversations from a distance.

3. Find out what the other computers on your network are up to.

4. Unleash your Raspberry Pi on the world.

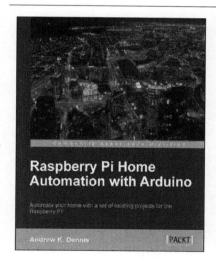

Raspberry Pi Home Automation with Arduino

ISBN: 978-1-84969-586-2   Paperback: 176 pages

Automate your home with a set of exciting projects for the Raspberry Pi

1. Learn how to dynamically adjust your living environment with detailed step-by-step examples.

2. Discover how you can utilize the combined power of the Raspberry Pi and Arduino for your own projects.

3. Revolutionize the way you interact with your home on a daily basis.

Please check **www.PacktPub.com** for information on our titles

Printed in Great Britain
by Amazon